Three Steps to Integrity: The ABC Model

Connecting How You Think, What You Do, Why You Do It, to Who You Are

William L. Jenkins

Three Steps to Integrity: The ABC Model
Connecting How You Think, What You Do, Why You Do It, to
Who You Are
by William L. Jenkins

Printed in the United States of America

ISBN 9781624197727

www.xulonpress.com

Contents

Integrity Deficit Disorder (IDD)

"If you have integrity, nothing else matters.
If you don't have integrity, nothing else matters."
~ Alan Simpson[28]

There has been no other time in the history of our nation and world when integrity has been so profoundly absent. The near collapse of the world economy in 2008 can be directly attributed to the lack of integrity in financial institutions and government. Today, we have yet to recover. Instead, we find increasing examples of vice, corruption, hypocrisy and greed in every institution of society. The pervasive and prolonged lack of integrity impacts you, your family and friends, your finances and career. I have given this cancer on our society a name: Integrity Deficit Disorder (IDD). It threatens to destroy our economy, the institutions we rely upon, and the very foundations of our society.

Does anyone care about integrity anymore? Most of us spend more time planning vacations than developing, striving for and guarding our integrity. Yet your integrity, who you are, is one of the most precious possessions you have. Similar to your good name, once you lose it, you may never regain it. There is no integrity insurance company that can indemnify you and no vaccine to immunize you against IDD.

The fact that you are reading this book gives me hope that integrity is not dead, it is just sleeping. We need to wake integrity up, and begin an integrity revival, making integrity the standard of character, not the exception. The best way to achieve integrity in your life and avoid IDD is to start on a journey that begins with a fresh new understanding of what integrity is.

Why another book on integrity?

Until now, no one has put a simple, comprehensive framework together that explains how all the components of integrity fit together and relate to each other. "Three Steps to Integrity: The ABC Model" goes farther than other integrity books because it explains an easy-to-understand framework, provides practical examples and tools, and offers steps for building a life of integrity. Plato, Socrates, and Aristotle dealt with the nature of ethics and integrity. Philosophers and theologians have written about integrity for centuries. Their books on the subject fill libraries. Even if you read every one of those books, you most likely will continue asking, "But what IS integrity?" and "Why should I even try to have integrity?" "Can I attain it if I do not have it?"

You are not alone. Ask ten people to define integrity and do not be surprised when you get ten different answers, commonly including:

• Beliefs	Honesty
• Character	Ideals
• Discipline	Principles
• Ethics	Trust
• Values	Virtues

If we cannot define integrity, then it is no wonder why so few achieve it!

While ethics and honesty are essential elements of integrity, integrity is more than any one, or group, of its parts. After reading "Three Steps to Integrity: The ABC Model", you will be able to identify the components of integrity; how they relate and complement each other; and most importantly, how to begin living a life of integrity, leading to wholeness, happiness and successful living.

The Integrity Network (eIntegrity.NET)

For those who wish to continue the journey to integrity with me and others, I invite you to visit our online community, The Integrity Network, at www.eIntegrity.NET. This forum makes it possible for those who value ethics, virtues, character and integrity to join forces and update the tools, resources and services for expanding integrity in our personal lives, families, workplaces, and society in general.

Conventions used in this book

The word "ethics" may be used as a singular entity or plural combination of its parts. Since I argue that ethics are the combination of beliefs, values principles and ideals, I use the convention of "ethics are" rather than "ethics is", unless quoting a source using ethics as a singular entity.

In formal writing, best practice is to use "one does" rather than "you do". Since the object of this book is to guide you on your personal quest to integrity, I intentionally use "you' and "your" throughout the book.

I document the sources used in writing this book as endnotes listed alphabetically by the author's last name. Therefore, the numbering scheme for citing sources is not sequential.

Acknowledgements

This book would not have been possible without the help and support of many people.

Thank you to my parents and siblings who planted the seeds of integrity in me over fifty years ago.

My family's support kept me writing when I hit the wall. My wife Anita gave me keen insights from her own character and integrity.

I want to especially acknowledge Brent Perkins and John Gordon Smith who patiently allowed me to test and revise my concepts. Bless you, both!

To the members of my congregation, who suffered through count-less sermons where I attempted to articulate and formulate "The ABC Model", you have my deepest appreciation.

To all my teachers, mentors, role models, and friends who have helped make me the person I am today, I thank you from my heart.

Dedication

To my wife, Anita,
Who is not only the world's best proofreader,
She is my love, my inspiration, my best friend,
And the closest example to excellence and integrity I know.

"The ABC Model" - Overview

To help illustrate "The ABC Model", I use three symbols: The circle represents your actions (A) or virtues. The triangle represents your beliefs (B), or ethics. The double headed arrow represents your character (C), including your habits and motivations, your moral fiber.

ACTIONS (VIRTUES) comprise the "A" Step to Integrity. Virtues are "WHAT you DO". We offer "The 10 Core Virtues" as a framework for virtuous living, grouped by moral, noble and spiritual virtues.

BELIEFS (ETHICS) comprise the "B" Step to Integrity. Ethics are "HOW you THINK". Ethics are the combination of your beliefs, values, principles and ideals.

CHARACTER composes the "C" Step to Integrity. Character deals with "WHY you DO it". Character is the "moral fiber" that stands between your actions and beliefs, connecting your ethics to your virtues. Character focuses on your habits and motives. Character exemplifies excellence, honor, leadership, commitment and responsibility.

INTEGRITY is the composite or wholeness of Actions, Beliefs and Character (ABC). Integrity is "WHO you ARE". Living your life of integrity provides tremendous benefits: wholeness, completeness, happiness, peace, success, abundance, and wisdom.

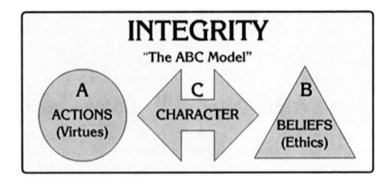

Ethics are how you think...
Virtues are what you do...
Character is why you do it...
Integrity is who you are!

Section One

Ethics: How You Think

"If moral behavior were simply following rules, we could program a computer to be moral."
~ Samuel P. Ginder[25]

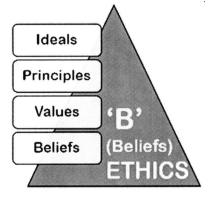

We begin the journey to integrity with ethics. Unfortunately, for many the journey also ends with ethics. That is why so many people never get to integrity. As important as ethics are to the structure of integrity, ethics mark just the first critical step on the pathway.

"Not so fast," you say. "I thought this was 'The ABC Model', and you are starting with 'B'." We begin with ethics (beliefs), because as Stephen Carter, in his book, *Integrity*, stated, the first step toward integrity is "discerning what is right and what is wrong"[1]. This first step is the most difficult step, because, as Carter noted, "All too many of us fall down on step [one]: we do not take the time to discern right from wrong. Indeed, I suspect that few of us really know just what we believe – what we value – and, often, we do not really want to know. Discernment is hard work; it

17

takes time and emotional energy. And it is so much easier to follow the crowd."[1]

In this section, we present a simple framework for developing a unified ethical system. Then we show how to relate those beliefs into virtuous actions, governed by the moral fiber of character. Only then is it possible to achieve integrity.

At the risk of oversimplification, while giving due diligence to the foundations laid by these great thinkers, I present at the beginning of each section a brief summary of the Greek philosopher whose contributions are essential to that step toward integrity.

- Section One: Ethics – Socrates
- Section Two: Virtues – Aristotle
- Section Three: Character - Plato

So we begin with ethics.

Socrates and ethics

Socrates (c. 469–399 B.C.) is best known for his contribution to ethics. One of the first Greek philosophers, Socrates encouraged society to turn their attention from the outside world to the inner person. Socrates left few writings. We see his teachings through his student Plato; who recorded his master's motto: "The unexamined life is not worth living for a human being."[28] His Socratic method entailed a series of questions to help determine fundamental beliefs (ethics). Socrates related knowledge to virtue, and virtue to happiness. A wise person knows and does what is right, and may achieve happiness.

"The ABC Model" subscribes to Socrates' emphasis upon the "examined life" as it relates to basic ethics, enabling you to understand, examine and relate your beliefs, values, principles and ideals.

What ethics are, and are not

The word ethics comes from the Greek word ethos. Merriam-Webster Dictionary[26] defines ethics as:

- A set of moral principles
- A theory or system of moral values

- The principles of conduct governing an individual or a group (professional ethics)
- A guiding philosophy

Stated simply, ethics are "the rules" and goals by which a person or organization bases standards for conduct. Your ethics specify the process by which you classify your beliefs, values, principles and ideals; determining how you conduct your life and pursue your goals.

"The ABC Model" presents ethics as the combination of four elements: beliefs, values, principles and ideals. In this section, we show how each element of ethics relates to the other components, and how the elements build upon each other.

The adage applies: "The whole is greater than the sum of its parts". Ethics are more than just the sum of these four elements. Synergy comes from analyzing and establishing a Code of Ethics for ourselves and organizations.

The first building block of your ethics is your beliefs, which form the foundation of all ethical systems. You do not have to be a religious person to have beliefs. From your beliefs, you develop values. Next, we show how principles emerge from your values. Each of the first three elements is reflective, looking inward. The final element, ideals, look forward to the person you want to be, the goals you want to achieve, the life you want to live.

The four components of ethics used in "The ABC Model" have synonyms that aid your understanding of their roles.

- Beliefs (rules)
- Values (preferences, priorities)
- Principles (moral compass)
- Ideals (goals, role models)

Ethics are internal, mental structures of the mind and spirit, as opposed to virtues, which are external actions. While you cannot see a person's ethics, you get a strong indication of what a person's ethics are by their actions.

Accordingly, ethics are "HOW you think". Note we do not mention ethics are "WHAT you think". It is not the intent of the author to dictate WHAT anyone should think. Ethics deal with the proper course of action based upon your set of beliefs, values, principles and ideals. By their precise nature, ethics are the branch of philosophy known as moral philosophy, or rational thinking about morality; including right or wrong, good or bad.

A discussion of morals makes some people uncomfortable. We live in a "live and let live" culture, where many frown upon making evaluative judgments of right and wrong. It is appropriate to mention, "making ethical judgments" is not the same as "being judgmental". Almost everyone makes ethical judgments each day. Ethics provide the framework for making those decisions regarding "right or wrong" and "good or bad" choices, actions, and habits.

Consequently, ethics serve as the basis of your ethical-moral framework. That framework is intimate and personal, but must be consistent with your actions and character if you are to achieve integrity. Again, I have no intention to tell anyone what their morals should be, or pass judgment upon anyone's moral character. This book presents a simple framework by which you may examine and improve your ethical-virtue system for consistency in achieving an excellent character and integrity.

Ethics ultimately answer the questions, "What should I do?" And "What ought I do with my life?" Supreme Court Justice Potter Stewart once said, "Ethics knows the difference between what you have a right to do and what is right to do."[28]

Examples of ethics

So how do you recognize ethics? Formal ethical structures may be contained in policies, laws or professional standards. Some of these examples are:

- Physicians' Hippocratic Oath
- Academic Honesty, Anti-Plagiarism Policy
- Protection of Intellectual Property
- Copyrights, Trademarks
- Codes of Conduct
- Statement of values
- Policies and Procedures
- Rights to Privacy, Medical Records
- Attorney Client Privilege

While these systems are necessary, they are difficult to translate into personal ethics. Many organizations go to enormous expense to develop their policies and procedures, but a majority of employees cannot explain what they are, if they have read them at all. This book presents a practical strategy for developing and implementing a comprehensive and consistent "Code of Character" into your daily personal and public life.

Why your ethics are important

You make decisions every day. Without ethics, your actions become erratic and purposeless at best. Ethics provide a means for deciding which course of action allows you to move toward your goals and ultimately to "happiness" and "success".

Socrates said a wise person knows and does what is right, and may achieve happiness. He established the underlying relationship between ethical knowledge, virtuous deeds and happiness. To the extent you act in harmony with your coherent ethical standards, you may successfully organize your values and principles to achieve your most important goals. In the Old Testament Book of Wisdom, the writer stated: "As a man thinks in his heart, so is he". (Proverbs 23:7) Ethics, in this context, include how you think in your innermost being. Those thoughts are critically relevant, as they ultimately determine who you are.

Your benefits and risks of ethics

We describe in Section Four the benefits of integrity: wholeness, happiness, completeness, wisdom, excellence, peace and success. Since ethics are the starting point for the life of integrity, ethics are your first step to those qualities of life. Ethics are essential for a happy, healthy, and successful life, including:

- Successful living. Ethics provide the only way to achieve authentic success. Ethical employees are honest, trustworthy, and loyal; qualities that have considerable value in the marketplace. People devoid of ethics ultimately fail because of their lack of positive character traits.
- Confidence. Knowing what you believe and why you believe it gives you more confidence in your personal and professional life.
- Authentic, meaningful life. Ethics provide a firm set of values and principles to guide your choices and decision-

making. With ethics, "cheating" or "cutting corners" are not in your life plan.
- Inner peace. Without a system of ethics, internal value conflicts are inevitable, making inner peace impossible. With ethics, an inner peace allows you to be more focused and productive.
- A reasoned core of beliefs.
- A set of values arising from your beliefs that become good daily habits.
- A principled life.
- A vision of the ideals you want in your life.

On the flipside, without ethics, a person or organization has no set boundaries for behavior. The lack of ethics in business leads to a culture of:

- Corruption
- Cutting corners
- Fragmentation
- Inconsistency
- Low morale
- Waste

As noted, Socrates said, "The unexamined life is not worth living". The danger is that most people do not take the time or energy to examine what they believe and why. A person without an ethical system is like a business without policies and procedures. Actions are in danger of becoming random, at times contradictory, and unethical, or worse - unlawful. Flaws in your ethics reduce your ability to be successful in reaching your goals.

How to create and apply your personal "Code of Ethics"
In the next four chapters, we address how to develop and implement a personal ethics system, offering real life suggestions for consideration. As we work through each component, we explain how to build a personal ethics framework.
The first step toward understanding and achieving integrity is establishing a consistent system of ethics, including beliefs, values, principles and ideals. This establishes a standard by which your actions and goals may be compared. Your ethical system

provides the rationale for both critical decisions and daily choices, helping you develop the habit of making the right choices. An ethical system should be dynamic, allowing for improvements and refinements as you develop and learn. While it is possible only to accept the ethical-belief system of an institution ("I am a Catholic", "I am a Libertarian"), the "unexamined life" is not enough. You must know what you believe and why you believe it!

Different individuals respond differently to ethical questions based upon the authority from which they base their beliefs (such as the Bible, The Party Platform, etc.), their culture or personal preferences. "Situation Ethics", an ethical theory developed by Episcopal priest Joseph Fletcher[7] in the 1960s, expands upon how different situations may elicit different ethical responses, such as "killing is prohibited, except as a soldier at war".

Another tool is a test Essex University devised to assess your attitude toward each of the following activities; with one point if you think it is never justified; two points if you think it is rarely justified; three if you view it as sometimes justified and four if you think it is always justified.

1. Avoiding paying the fare on public transport.
2. Cheating on taxes if you have a chance.
3. Driving faster than the speed limit.
4. Keeping money found in the street.
5. Lying in your own interests.
6. Not reporting accidental damage you have done to a parked car.
7. Throwing away litter in a public place.
8. Driving under the influence of alcohol.
9. Making up information on a job application.
10. Buying something you know is stolen.

According to the authors, a score of 10 or below suggests you are very honest, 11 to 15 means you do not mind bending the rules but are more honest than average, 16 to 20 suggests you are relaxed about the rules and anything more than 21 suggests you do not believe in living by the rules.[27] These exercises help quantify your ethics and enable objective reflection upon how your actions match your ethical-belief system. If you say you believe one thing, but do another, then there is no integrity to your ethical virtue system.

Why ethics training is not enough

In the aftermath of the 2008 financial and political crises, many agencies began requiring "ethics training" for their employees. Ethics training usually involves a review and interpretation of the laws, policies, and rules. So, while important, ethics training alone is doomed to failure if not translated into living out the beliefs, values, principles and ideals of the ethical system into virtuous actions through high moral character. In other words, ethics stop short of integrity because ethics focus on knowing and keeping the rules; not how to do and be a person of integrity.

Chapter 1

Beliefs: Rules You Live By

"This is how humans are: we question all our beliefs,
except for the ones we really believe, and those we
never think to question."
~ Orson Scott Card[30]

Have you ever stopped to analyze what you believe and why you believe it? Have you asked yourself where you obtained your core beliefs? Beliefs are the rules and assumptions accumulated from parents, teachers, religion, society, and so on. As you will see, beliefs are essential to your understanding of truth, good and reality. You should take the time and effort to reflect upon your beliefs in the larger context of ethics and integrity. Of course, a person may hold thousands of beliefs. Our focus is upon core beliefs, or beliefs that are the basis of other beliefs. Beliefs are your roadmap of reality. Beliefs are the way you perceive everything in life, making your beliefs a vital part of your life.

In this chapter, we offer some resources for creating an inventory of your core beliefs, including a fresh look at the authority of your beliefs, and analyze why you believe what you say you believe.

The Answer Man

I remember how naive I was after graduating from a state college and planning to go to seminary. I imagined that after another three years of study, not only would I have a master's degree, but

I would have all my beliefs confirmed or refined. I would have an answer for every possibly question; I would become "the answer man". A wise professor broke that illusion when he said, "Seminary is not a place where you find an answer to every question. You will be blessed, after three years, if you discover all the questions, much less the answers. The answers come throughout a lifetime, if at all." Discovering and refining your beliefs is hard work. There are no easy answers. It requires hard work and honest soul searching.

Beliefs are often relegated to religious beliefs, but even atheists have beliefs – one of which is God does not exist. In examination, belief is as much a part of the scientific method as religion. Both hypotheses and theorems are simply beliefs that await evidence or verification. Scientists believe in the Big Bang Theory, atheists believe there is no God, agnostics believe it makes no difference if there is a God or not and the religious/spiritual person believes in the Divine. Whether religious or secular, we all live by beliefs. Dr. Leonard Mlodinow in the 2011 book, *War of the Worldviews: Sciences versus Spirituality*, said "We make decisions about what is true and what is false, but most of us rarely think about how we come to our beliefs."[18] [Note: Dr. Mlodinow took the side of the science worldview over Dr. Deepak Chopra's spiritual worldview.]

What beliefs are, and are not

We define beliefs as:

- What a person believes or assumes to be "the truth".
- The framework from which to develop your understanding of "right and wrong".
- The conviction of the truth of some statement especially when based on evaluation of evidence.
- A state of mind in which you place trust or confidence in a tenet or body of tenets.[25]

Beliefs are not, however:

- Being law-abiding - keeping rules is not the same as being ethical.

- Feelings - many people tend to equate ethics with their feelings.
- Doing whatever society accepts.
- Religion - Most religions, of course, advocate high ethical standards. Yet if ethics are limited to religion, then ethics would apply only to religious people.

Examples of belief systems

- The Scientific Method
- The Ten Commandments
- The Golden Rule
- The Big Bang Theory
- The U.S. Constitution
- Codes of Ethics
- Creeds
- Doctrines
- Evolution
- Laws
- Axioms, such as "All people are created equal"
- Truisms, such as "Let your conscience be your guide", "To thine own self be true", "Live and let live", etc.

Why beliefs are important

Since beliefs are what you perceive to be the truth, they play a key role in your overall moral-ethical structure. For example, a belief that you hold as truth will affect your virtue of truthfulness. You use your beliefs to navigate the uncertainties of the world around you. Beliefs influence how you interpret reality. Once you interpret reality through your beliefs, it becomes difficult to see other realities, unless you refine your set of beliefs. Beliefs have within them the power to enable you to do good and the power to destroy. Your beliefs shape the framework that guides your understanding of all your life events.

The benefits and risks of beliefs

Mahatma Gandhi once said people "often become what they believe themselves to be. If I believe I cannot do something, it makes me incapable of doing it. But when I believe I can, then I acquire the ability to do it even if I did not have it in the beginning."[28]

27

The dangers of beliefs include:

- A person may genuinely believe something that is incorrect!
- Not having a reflective system of beliefs means you will be more likely to act impulsively or inconsistently.
- A belief system may become a dogma or ideology that justifies evil (terrorism, Nazism, racism, etc.).

How to establish beliefs

Beliefs form in a variety of ways. From the moment of your birth, developing a belief structure begins. You tend to assimilate the beliefs of the people around you, especially your parents and teachers. Many individuals believe religious tenets taught in childhood. Political beliefs often reflect those of the majority of the community. Selection of your friends and associates may be one of your most consequential decisions, because friends influence both your beliefs and behavior.

While there is nothing wrong with assimilating the belief structures of institutions (the "platform" of a political party, the doctrines of a church, etc.) it is necessary to ask "Why?" you believe what you believe. No particular belief exists in isolation. Beliefs always connect and relate to other beliefs. Sincere analysis of both what you believe and why you believe it is the essential first step toward integrity.

Tools for analyzing your beliefs

Once you define your core beliefs, you may test them against:

- Reason – does it make sense?
- Experience – does it coincide with other experiences?
- Authority – by what authority is the belief based?
- Consistency – is the belief consistent with other beliefs and actions?

How beliefs fit into the integrity framework

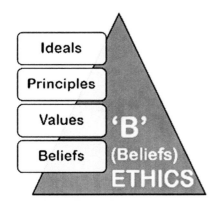

Beliefs and values

While beliefs are truths about what is right and wrong, values are "what you like, and the order in which you like them". Beliefs roll up into values.

Beliefs and principles

Values translate into principles that help guide your actions. Principles exist whether you follow them or not.

Beliefs and ideals

Ideals are the goals you set, the life you aspire to live and the person you strive to become, all rooted in your beliefs.

Chapter 2

Values: What You Prize

"It's not hard to make decisions when you
know what your values are."
~ Roy Disney, Walt Disney Companies[28]

Values are the things you like, and the order in which you like them. If you want to know what your values are, look at your check stubs! What you spend your money and time on is probably what you most value. Values emerge from your beliefs. For instance, if you believe in getting ahead at any cost, then you probably prize money, and the things it can buy; the outward signs of what the world calls success. Hypocrisy, the opposite of integrity, emerges when you say you believe one thing but value or do the opposite thing. For example, many say they believe in family values, but fail to demonstrate family values with those dearest to them.

Old fashioned values

Old fashioned values are the common, traditional values prevalent in the United States during the 1940s and 1950s; such as God, country, family and morality. I grew up on a farm near Yazoo City, Mississippi and came of age in the late 1950s and 1960s. We had to pump water from a well, cook on a wood burning stove, feed the chickens, slop the hogs, and harvest a dozen crops that kept us fed throughout the year. We had no electricity or telephone, and there was that matter of the "outdoor bathroom".

We were a large, poor family. I never thought we were poor, because we were rich in the things that matter; in the things that money cannot buy. Those values included family, love, faith, and hope for a brighter tomorrow. That is where I first learned what old fashioned values were.

What values are, and are not

Values may be defined as broad preferences concerning appropriate courses of action. As such, values indicate a person's sense of right and wrong, or what "ought" to be. This "oughtness" is an essential aspect of ethics. Dr. Christopher Panza said, "To take ethics – or the investigation of what ought to be – seriously is to engage head on with the question of value."[20]

A personal value is an assumption upon which principles can be collected. A value system is a set of consistent values and principles. A core value is a foundation upon which to build other values and principles of integrity. Values emerge from your core beliefs regarding what is right and fair in terms of your actions and your interactions with others. Values are what you believe to be of worth (value-able) and importance to your life.

Values are subjective and vary from individual to individual and across cultures. Values influence attitudes and behavior.

Examples of values

Types of values include ethical/moral values, religious/political values, social values, and aesthetic values.

Here is a list of common values:

- Knowledge (education)
- Family associations (love, duty, loyalty, support)
- Happiness
- Health
- Life
- Liberty
- Truth
- Beauty

Why values are important

Knowing your personal values is extremely valuable because your values shape everything about you. Values are influencing every aspect of your life, even if you cannot name them all. Your values help design the plan of your whole life. Personal values provide an internal reference for what is right, beneficial, important, useful, etc.

Values are important because over time the public expression of individual values lays the foundations of laws, customs and traditions. Values generate behavior and help solve common problems by comparative rankings of value, the results of which provide answers to questions of why people do what they do and in what order they choose to do them. A culture is a community that shares a set of common values, which establish social expectations. Without personal values, there would be no cultural reference against which to measure the virtue of individual values, and cultural identity would disintegrate.

The benefits and risks of values

Values are standards and qualities you consider beneficial or desirable in life. They vary from person to person because they depend on individual judgment.

Your values influence your:

- Relationships
- Behavior
- Choices
- Personal identity

How to establish values

Values arise in many different ways. The most influential element for building values is a person's family and friends. The family is responsible for teaching children what is right and wrong long before there are other influences. As a child starts school, the learning process helps to develop the values of children. A family's religion or spirituality plays a role in teaching a child the right and wrong behaviors.

How to determine your values

Reserve some quiet time to reflect without interruption or disturbance. Ask yourself "What is most important to my life?" Write down your answers. Use simple phrases (such as your relationship with family, spirituality, happiness, retirement at 55) and do not focus on the order at this point. Choose the things you find truly foremost in your life. Do not write down values you think you should have, if they are not essential to you. Also, this list should not be a "bucket list" (things you want to do before you die) unless that item is actually a value of considerable importance. The list should contain a dozen or so of your core values. Remember, these are your values.

The Values Calculator
Next, prioritize your list of values. An excellent way to do this is to identify the first two values on your list. Then ask yourself if you could have only one of the two, which would it be? Next, go to the following two values, and determine which one is most important. When finished, you should have a set of high priority and lower priority values. Conduct a second round of one-to-one analyses on both sets, much like in a double-elimination tournament bracket, until you have determined your highest value. You may be surprised how your values prioritize themselves.

Examine your values
Once you have a prioritized values list, examine your values closely. Are there any that do not fit? Are there any you would like to change? This may mean dropping a value, adding a value, or tweaking your priorities. Regularly review and modify your list of values as circumstances change.

Here is an example of "Top 10 Personal Values" (listed alphabetically):

1. Balance in life
2. Benevolence
3. Devotion to family and/or friends
4. Fun & Joy
5. Non-hypocritical, authentic living
6. Happiness
7. Health and wholeness
8. Justice
9. Knowledge
10. Spirituality

Evaluate how your values should affect your life
Finally, think through how your list of values affects your life. If these are the things that are most valuable to you, how should

they guide your decisions? If you think you are not following your values in your life, you have the ability to change. Your list of values becomes a resource to evaluate any decision with confidence by asking yourself: "What should I do in this situation if these are my guiding values in life?" Apply this method to every area of your life and you will surely see your life becoming more aligned with your values. As your situation changes, update your values as needed. Adapting to changes in life will be crucial to your success in accomplishing your goals. These values should help guide in making the necessary decisions about your principles, goals, and the things you are willing to sacrifice.

> "Try not to become a [person] of success but rather try to
> become a [person] of value."
> ~ Albert Einstein[28]

How values fit into the integrity framework

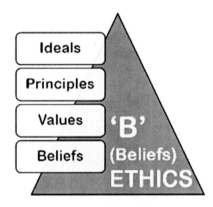

Values and beliefs

Beliefs are the rules you say you live by. Values are the things you value in life, and the order in which you value them. Beliefs are rules for behavior, while values determine what should be judged as good or evil in specific situations.

Values and principles

Your value system is a set of consistent values, or prioritized likes and dislikes. Principles emerge from your values as your morals. Principles exist whether you follow them or not.

Values and ideals

Values allow you to connect the things you value with your goals for your life, bringing consistency to your life.

Chapter 3

Principles:
Your Moral Compass

"Rules are not necessarily sacred, principles are."
~ Franklin D. Roosevelt[28]

What principles are, and are not

Principles are fundamental truths derived from your beliefs and values that shape your moral framework or code of conduct. A value is only as valuable as a person places importance upon it, but a principle is essential even if you try to ignore it exists. In other words, principles exist whether you follow them or not. Failure to follow principles comes with consequences.

Stephen Covey[4], author of *The 7 Habits of Highly Effective People*, says principles are external natural laws, while values remain internal and subjective. Covey proclaims that values govern people's behavior, but principles ultimately determine the consequences. Covey's "character ethic" aligns values with "universal and timeless" principles. Covey added: "Correct principles are like compasses: they are always pointing the way. And if we know how to read them, we won't get lost, confused, or fooled by conflicting voices and values. Principles are self-evident, self-validating natural laws. They don't change or shift. They provide 'true north' direction to your life when navigating the 'streams' of your environments. Principles apply at all time in all places. They surface in the form of values, ideas, norms, and teachings that uplift, ennoble, fulfill, empower, and inspire people. The lesson of history is that to the degree people and civilizations have operated in harmony with correct principles, they have prospered."[4]

Michael Josephson, law professor and founder of the Josephson Institute of Ethics, said, "We translate values into principles so they can guide and motivate ethical conduct. Ethical principles are the rules of conduct that derive from ethical values."[11]

Examples of principles

So what are some examples of principles? It is easy to confuse principles with virtues and ideals, depending on how you define them. However, virtues and ideals coincide with principles.

Examples of general personal and professional principles include:

1. Accountability (taking responsibility)
2. Avoidance of conflicts of interest
3. Benevolence (doing good)
4. Commitment (fidelity, duty)
5. Compliance with the laws, codes of conduct, regulations
6. Confidentiality (respect for privacy)
7. Excellence (due diligence)
8. Fairness (impartiality)
9. Preventing harm
10. Reliability (keep your promises, word and commitments)
11. Respect for the autonomy and well-being of others
12. Transparency (openness, honesty)

Principles of professional ethics

Individuals acting as professionals take on an additional burden of ethical responsibility, such as medicine, law, accounting, or engineering. These written codes provide rules of conduct and standards of behavior based on the principles of professional ethics. Even when not written into a code, principles of professional ethics are expected of people in business, employees, volunteers, elected representatives and so on.

Ethix.org offers the following model:

Ten Principles of Highly Ethical Business Leaders

1. **Treat all employees as unique individuals.**
   Don't reduce people to a utility — a means to achieve your ends.
2. **Support each person's freedom to grow and develop.**
   Never judge anyone through stereotypes, or as fixed and unchangeable.
3. **Communicate to people by name with respect.**
   Never use hurtful labels or refer to a person by his or her job function.
4. **Model and encourage a balanced life of good work and rest.**
   Don't make long-term demands on employees that undermine balanced lives.
5. **Honor and respect families of others.**
   Don't forget that each person lives in a broader context beyond his or her work.
6. **Value life, safety, and health.**
   Work processes or products should not create unnecessary risk or harm.
7. **Keep your promises.**
   Don't violate written or verbal commitments, or look for loopholes to do so.
8. **Be fair and just in financial matters.**
   Don't tolerate unfair wages, prices, or financial practices.
9. **Communicate honestly and truthfully.**
   Never misrepresent people, products, services, or facts.
10. **Recognize the accomplishments of others.**
    Don't claim the success of others for yourself.

"All I Really Need to Know" principles

Robert Fulghum, in his often quoted book, *All I Really Need to Know I Learned in Kindergarten*[8], offers another way of viewing some basic principles for living.

"All I really need to know about how to live and what to do and how to be I learned in kindergarten. Wisdom was not at the top of the graduate school mountain, but there in the sand pile at school."

"These are the things I learned:

- Share everything.
- Play fair.
- Don't hit people.
- Put things back where you found them.
- Clean up your own mess.
- Don't take things that aren't yours.
- Say you're sorry when you hurt somebody.
- Wash your hands before you eat.
- Flush.
- Warm cookies and cold milk are good for you.
- Live a balanced life - learn some and think some and draw and paint and sing and dance and play and work every day some.
- Take a nap every afternoon.
- When you go out in the world, watch out for traffic, hold hands and stick together.
- Be aware of wonder. Remember the little seed in the Styrofoam cup: the roots go down and the plant goes up and nobody really knows how or why, but you are like that.
- Goldfish and hamsters and white mice and even the little seed in the Styrofoam cup - they all die. So do you.
- And then remember the Dick-and-Jane books and the first word you learned - the biggest word of all - LOOK."

"Everything you need to know is in there somewhere. The Golden Rule and love and basic sanitation. Ecology and politics and equality and sane living. Take any one of those items and extrapolate it into sophisticated adult terms and apply it to your family life or your work or government or your world and it holds true and clear and firm. Think what a better world it would be if we all - the whole world - had cookies and milk at about 3 o'clock in the afternoon and then lay down with your blankie for a nap. Or if all governments had as a basic policy to always put things back where they found them and to clean up their own mess. And it is still true; no matter how old you are, when you go out in the world, it is best to hold hands and stick together."[8]

Why principles are important

Principles are significant because they provide the means to clarify how your beliefs and values relate to your actions. If, as Stephen Covey asserts, principles are like your moral compass, then the absence of principles leaves you like a ship without the ability to navigate. President Dwight Eisenhower said, "A people who value its privileges above its principles soon lose both."[28] The great comedian, Red Skelton, put it well: "Our principles are the springs of our actions. Our actions [are] the springs of our happiness or misery. Too much care, therefore, cannot be taken in forming our principles."[28]

The benefits and risks of principles

James Kouzes[13] and Barry Posner[22], in *The Leadership Challenge* wrote: "When you clarify the principles that will govern your life and the ends that you will seek, you give purpose to your daily decisions. A personal creed gives you a point of reference for navigating the sometimes stormy seas of organizational life. Without a set of such beliefs, your life has no rudder, and you're easily blown about by the winds of fashion. A credo to guide you prevents confusion on the journey. The internal resolution of competing beliefs also leads to personal integrity, which is essential to believability. A leader with integrity has one self, at home and at work, with family and colleagues. Such a leader has a unifying set of values that guide choices of action regardless of the situation."[13]

The benefits of principles include:

- Purpose to your daily decisions.
- A point of reference for navigating the sometimes-stormy seas.
- A credo to guide and prevent confusion.
- Principles uplift, ennoble, fulfill, empower, and inspire people.
- Proven track to success.

The risk of ignoring a principle is like ignoring gravity - while you are falling, you can pretend the principle does not exist; but eventually you pay the consequences.

How to build principles

Principles are finite, fewer in number than values, since principles are more universal and may cover multiple values and beliefs. Individuals do not create principles. They are external natural laws you discover as you go through life. You may elect to implement principles in your life, requiring you to extract rules of conduct from beliefs and values. Doing so enables you to become principled, or an individual who habitually bases actions on principles.

As noted, Stephen Covey's "character ethic" aligns personal values with "universal and timeless" principles. Character ethics assume there are principles that exist in all people. Principles have universal applications, and are different from practices, which are for specific situations.

Covey[4] offers the "Seven Habits" to apply principles and character:

1. Be proactive.
2. Begin with the end in mind.
3. Put first things first.
4. Think win/win.
5. Seek first to understand, then to be understood.
6. Synergize.
7. Sharpen the saw.

How principles fit into the integrity framework

Principles and beliefs

Beliefs and values are internal and subjective components of ethics. Principles are external natural laws of ethics. Beliefs and principles relate to each other in that values spring from beliefs, and principles emerge from your values. When there are contradictions in your beliefs and principles, there is discord and no possibility of integrity.

Principles and values

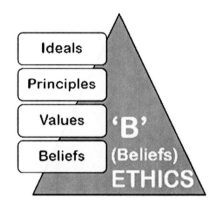

A value is only significant if you as a person place importance upon it, but a principle is essential even if you try to ignore its existence. Principles are external natural laws, while values remain internal and subjective. For example, you may try to ignore the principle of accountability and may even develop strategies and techniques for living without being accountable, but you will have to cope with conflict, inconsistency and self-contradiction which destroy the hope of attaining integrity.

Principles and ideals

Different cultures have varying values. You may suffer from the societal consequences if you ignore a shared value. You may suffer financial loss, physical harm, imprisonment or even death as a result of the societal consequences of rejecting the shared values of the society in which you live.

If you are serious about developing personal integrity, you need to identify the principles that define your objectives, goals and ideals.

Chapter 4

Ideals: Who You Ought To Be

"Ideals are like stars: you will not succeed in touching
them with your hands, but like the seafaring man on the
desert of waters, you choose them as your guides,
and following them you reach your destiny."
~ Carl Schurz[28]

There is an old saying, "If you are aiming at nothing, you
will probably hit it." Ideals and goals are critical for success. Collectively, your ideals and goals form your roadmap for
achieving success, happiness, and integrity. They reveal your
life's vision statement (what your life "ought" to be). Remember,
ethics is about "oughtness".

The other components of ethics (beliefs, values, principles)
require looking inward, reflectively, and in some sense to past
experiences. Ideals discover the wealth of those reflections and
look forward to the future; to the person you want to be and the
things you want to accomplish.

Oseola McCarty

It is essential to have good role models. I had the good fortune
of knowing some incredible people who were excellent examples
of character and integrity. Some were famous; others lived lives of
quiet courage and honor with genuine humility.

I did not personally know Miss Oseola McCarty, but she
remains one of my favorite heroes. Miss McCarty was a humble

washerwoman in Hattiesburg, Mississippi. She dropped out of school as a girl to care for an ailing aunt. She never married or had a family of her own. She never owned a car, and walked everywhere she went, except when friends drove her to church each Sunday.

What was remarkable about Miss McCarty was her frugality. She put a small amount from her earnings aside into her savings account, (nickels, dimes and quarters) from every load of clothes. In July 1995, Miss McCarty asked her banker how much money she had in her account. Surprised to see how large her savings and interest had grown, and true to her humble nature, she said, "What does an eighty year old woman do with that much money?" She decided to give $150,000 to the University of Southern Mississippi so deserving students will have the opportunity she never had. She never sought fame for her benevolence. However, she appeared on the Tonight Show. President Clinton bestowed upon her the Presidential Citizens Medal (the nation's second highest civilian honor), and she received the first honorary doctorate ever awarded by USM.

Growing up poor in the poorest region of the country, my parents instilled in each of my brothers, sisters and me that we could achieve whatever we set out to do. The ideal of getting an excellent education came from my parents' values. They worked long hours to make sure we had a solid foundation in education, faith and family.

This chapter helps understand the importance of ideals, offering some practical suggestions on how to prepare and achieve your life goals, including your life's mission statement (how you plan to achieve your dream).

What ideals are, and are not

The Latin word from which we get "ideal" combines the meanings of "perfect" and "idea". Ideals are standards or models of excellence. An ideal is a principle or value that you actively seek as a goal. Ideals are particularly valuable in ethics, as setting ideals increases the likelihood you will strive for and achieve your goals.

Examples of ideals
It may be useful to envision examples of ideals in categories.

Examples of political ideals include:

- Life
- Liberty (Freedom)
- Pursuit of Happiness

Examples of spiritual ideals include:

- Love
- Joy
- Peace
- Kindness
- Patience
- Gentleness
- Self-control

Examples of moral ideals:

- Truth
- Fairness (Equality)
- Duty
- Honor

Examples of personal ideals:

- Wholeness
- Completeness
- Wisdom
- Abundance
- Success
- Peace
- Happiness

The benefits and risks of ideals
Individuals create personal goals to achieve ideals. For example, a student sets the goal to earn a degree. An athlete works to win the championship. A traveler plans to cruise around

the world. Financial goals help us plan for retirement or to make a significant purchase. On a personal level, ideals help you identify and work toward your own ideals; most often personal, financial or career-based goals. Ideals include both long-term and short-term goals. Short-term goals are often stepping stones, or intermediate steps, toward achieving a long term goal. In all areas of your personal life, managing goals generates enormous dividends. Knowing exactly what you need to achieve, and who you want to be, defines what you should concentrate upon, helping prioritize your goals. Ideals and goal-setting promote a long-term vision and short-term motivation, helping manage your resources in working toward the goals. It helps resolve internal conflicts that often sabotage our efforts.

In ethics, each person should strive to become more of an ideal person. You measure character by examining how closely you live up to your ideal self. Your belief in the ability to achieve a personal ideal affects that effort. Achieving ideals requires focus and long-term commitment. Success requires emotional maturity. The large picture involves many small, day-to-day efforts. However, be careful. Implementing ideals and resolving conflicting ideals often reduce ideals to ideology, dogma, or a group of beliefs to which adherents must slavishly follow.

How to establish ideals

As a child, you began to learn to model behavior and life after those you admire. That starts with your parents or older siblings. Soon you develop heroes from cartoons, television, movies, sports, etc. Sometimes those role models disappoint, but strong role models mentor you toward achieving your full potential. Growing older, you develop the ability to see ideal models in less tangible, but critically esteemed abstractions, such as love, fidelity, and honesty. Your ideals are intensely personal. They are the product of your soul and spirit. No one can tell you what or who your ideals should be. You discover the genuine ideals as you experience the joys and sorrows of life.

One exercise that may help in identifying your ideals is to write down the names of the people you most admire, and then identify the character traits they exemplify that makes you admire them. Those qualities will help form the basis for your ideals. Look at the list of examples we offer and build your personalized list of the ideals you most want in your life.

Ideals as personal strategic planning

Another way to think of ideals is personal strategic planning. Just as businesses and organizations do long range strategic planning, your ideals help guide your decision making, priorities, and measure your progress toward life goals. This combines the elements of mission (what you do), vision (who you want to be), values (the things you hold as valuable), and strategy (the measures of means and ends to achieve your goals).

How ideals fit into "The ABC Model" integrity framework

Ideals and beliefs

Your basic beliefs influence what you determine to be ideal. The goals you set, the life you aspire to live and the person you strive to become, are all rooted in your beliefs.

Ideals and values

Ideals are similar to values in that you prioritize them. Depending upon their definition, values may become ideals.

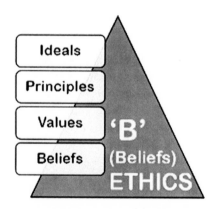

Ideals and principles

Sometimes, ideals and principles may conflict with each other. In such circumstances, one must take priority. For example, a judge often must settle between the ideal of truth and the ideal of fairness. The French Revolution raised the principles of "Liberty, Equality, Brotherhood" to the importance of ideals. Most political and religious movements have a number of ideals. An ideal is a principle or value that you actively seek as a goal.

46

Ideals and virtue

A virtue is an ideal that you can "do", or make a habit. For example, the ideal of duty requires daily attention to responsibilities and details that insure you meet all your obligations. You do not cut corners, procrastinate, or take the easy way out. By doing so, you develop the habit of duty.

Section Two

Virtues: What You Do

"All the gold which is under or upon the earth is not
enough to give in exchange for virtue."
~ Plato[25]

Having presented the basics of ethics (how you think), we now focus on virtues (what you do). Ethics (beliefs, values, principles and ideals) are all internal mental concepts; virtues are external behaviors that put your ethics into action. Virtues are expressions of your moral principles. There should be consistency between your ethics and virtues. "Your walk should match your talk!" Translating ethics into action is a function of your character, which we consider in the next section. With practice, virtues become habits that define your character.

For example, you may subscribe to an ethical system similar to the Ten Commandments. Your ethics indicate that you do certain things, such as "love your neighbor as yourself" and not do others. But you have a neighbor you find quite unlovable. Until you put the ethic of "love your neighbor" into action, as a virtue,

49

there is no connection or consistency between your beliefs and your actions. That is why many find it easier to be consistent with "Thou shalt not" than "Thou shalt". The former does not require an action except abstinence; the latter requires an overt effort, which is always demanding.

We match the three classic Greek philosophers to each of the "Three Steps to Integrity: The ABC Model"; Aristotle for virtues, Socrates for ethics, and Plato for character. Of course, all three philosophers addressed ethics, virtues and character. One in particular is the champion of each step of "The ABC Model". We present the teachings in particularly simple, easy to understand language that will help illustrate the essential basics.

Aristotle and virtues

We begin with Aristotle. Aristotle (c. 384–322 B.C.), a student of Plato and teacher of Alexander the Great, was the first to develop a comprehensive system of Western philosophy. Aristotle considered ethics to be a practical discipline, mastered by doing rather than simply reasoning. In his *Nichomachean Ethics*, he defines what is now commonly called virtue ethics.

Without getting too deeply into Greek Philosophy, Aristotle defined a virtue as a morally good habit or trait that assists in building personal character. Accordingly, Aristotle held that virtues are moral excellence: behaviors based on high moral standards, striving for what he identified as "the good".

Hence, virtues are excellence at being human; discovering the skills that help us live, form meaningful relationships, succeed, and ultimately find what Aristotle called "eudaimonia", happiness, or the best life.

Aristotle used two terms that are crucial in understanding his philosophy of virtues: "the good" and "the golden mean". In short, "the good" includes those things desirable in an excellent human life; and "the mean" is the optimum point between two extremes of behavior.

Aristotle's "The Good"

A virtue allows you to achieve "the good" in life. Aristotle began with the principal idea that you must decide what is best for you as a human being. Ethics, he insisted, are not an academic exercise. Ethics ask what "the good" is for human beings because you will be better able to achieve your good if you develop a fuller understanding of what it takes to excel.

Aristotle did not specify a list of goods. He assumed anyone may simply arrange a personal list of good habits or traits. For example, it is good to be well, have friends, achieve goals, and to demonstrate such virtues as temperance, justice, prudence and courage.

Aristotle assumed that the highest good is desirable for itself, and no other reason. In other words, do the good because it is the good. Striving for "the good" leads to happiness and living well. Aristotle held happiness as the ultimate goal in life. For Aristotle, self-realization is the surest path to happiness. He taught to achieve happiness and joy that permeate the good life; requires living a balanced life and avoiding excesses.

Aristotle's "Golden Mean"

Aristotle defined a moral virtue as expressions of character that are "the golden mean" between two extremes of a trait or habit (the deficit and the excess). For example, charity is the golden mean between being a miser and being extravagantly wasteful; bravery is the mean virtue between the two extremes of cowardice and recklessness. Finding the golden mean requires common sense (prudence).

Today, we might call the golden mean "the sweet spot" between too much and too little of a virtue. The extreme constitutes a vice. So every virtue has at least two vices: too much or too little of "the good" thing. That does not always mean the exact middle between the deficit and the excess.

In "The ABC Model", an ethic is a thought or belief, and a virtue is an action. Therefore, an ethic, in that sense, cannot also be a virtue. "The ABC Model" adapts Aristotle's understanding of virtues as moral excellence, adding a template for doing the right thing, for the right reason, in the right way, at the right time.

The 10 Core Virtues

How many virtues are there? We have identified at least forty, but we offer "The 10 Core Virtues" as a foundation for all other virtues which plays a key role in developing your character and ability to achieve integrity.

Our focus is upon these traditional virtues, which form the basis for all other virtues. Plato believed that different virtues cannot exist independently. They are all interconnected, and either increase or impede each other. It is necessary, therefore, that you strive for wholeness in virtues. These virtues organize into three groups: the traditional four moral virtues, three noble virtues, and three spiritual virtues. Others refer to what we call noble virtues as ethical virtues. Because "The ABC Model" identifies ethics as a separate entity, we chose the term noble to minimize confusion.

Deficit (vice)	Virtue ("Golden Mean")	Excess (vice)
The 10 Core Virtues		
The Moral Virtues		
Corruption	1. **Justice**	Unfairness
Insensibility	2. **Temperance**	Self-indulgence, Gluttony
Foolishness	3. **Prudence**	Over-cautious
Cowardice	4. **Courage**	Rashness
The Noble Virtues		
Dishonesty	5. **Honesty**	Boastfulness
Suspicion, Distrust	6. **Trust**	Gullible, Blind Trust
Sloth, Apathy	7. **Discipline**	Obsession, Compulsion
The Spiritual Virtues		
Doubt, Anxiety	8. **Faith**	Blind Faith, Over-confidence
Despair, Cynicism	9. **Hope**	Presumption, False Hope
Indifference, Ingratitude	10. **Charity (agape)**	Greed, Wastefulness

Why your virtues are important

How is it that people can employ such things as Ponzi schemes; athletes using illegal drugs, or governors trying to sell Senate seats? What are murderers, child molesters and thieves thinking? There is no consistency between what they espouse and how they behave. They convince themselves "The rules do NOT apply to me!" They rationalize:

- The law, either moral or civil, does not pertain to me; or
- Even if it is "wrong" for others, it is "not wrong" for me; or
- I am smarter than other people and will get away with it; or
- No one will ever find it out.

It all comes down to choices. You make them every day. Either you live by the rules, or you do not. When you do not, you and potentially many others suffer the consequences. Stop to think, in your personal life, who would suffer from a total breakdown in your integrity? Who would you be affecting besides yourself? Possibly these include your spouse, your children, your parents/siblings, your friends and co-workers? Seldom can you fail at integrity and be the only one to suffer.

The Hebrew word for speaking and acting is the same word. Until your words (ethics) and actions (virtues) align, you have no integrity. In the Bible, James said, "Be doers of the word and not just hearers only." (James 1:22). He goes on to say, "Faith (beliefs) without works (virtuous actions) is dead." (James 2:20).

How to discover and apply your virtues to real life

In the next chapters, we offer "The 10 Core Virtues" in three groups: Moral, Noble and Spiritual Virtues. As we look at each virtue, you will be able to identify the deficiency vice and excess vice of each. Discovering and implementing these virtues will provide the foundation for living a life of virtues, with character and integrity.

As you proceed through these virtues, ask yourself how you are, or are not, expressing these traits in your life. By doing so, your focus will allow virtues to grow and mature in your life.

Chapter 5

Your Moral Virtues

"The greatest virtues are those which
are most useful to other persons."
~ Aristotle[25]

"The ABC Model" organizes "The 10 Core Virtues" into three groupings: Moral, Noble, and Spiritual Virtues.

MORAL VIRTUES	NOBLE	SPIRITUAL VIRTUES
Justice	Honesty	Faith
Temperance	Trust	Hope
Prudence	Discipline	Love
Courage		

The Greek philosophers identified four moral virtues, (sometimes called cardinal virtues) that are the core of moral living. They are justice, temperance, prudence and courage. These moral virtues are necessary for all other virtues to exist.

Four Virtuous Norms
We interpret these virtues as easily understood guides for everyday life, and match them to what we recognize as the "Four

Virtuous Norms": (Doing the right thing, in the right way, at the right time, for the right reason).

- **Justice** promotes fairness, especially for the poor and powerless. It rewards good and punishes evil, balancing the scales of justice, without which society descends into corruption. Justice provides the first virtuous norm: "**Doing the right thing**".
- **Temperance** is the virtue of moderation and balance. It guards against excesses. Temperance supplies the second virtuous norm: "Doing the right thing, **in the right way**".
- **Prudence** is common sense and wisdom. It is the ability to know when to do or say something. Prudence fulfills the third virtuous norm: "Doing the right thing, in the right way, **at the right time**".
- **Courage** is the ability to "hang in there" in those times when the going gets tough. It is the fortitude that allows you the courage to do the right thing no matter what the cost. Courage fulfills the fourth virtuous norm: "Doing the right thing, in the right way, at the right time, **for the right reason**".

Virtues are choices to habitually do what is good. You must work to develop and maintain moral virtues.

Justice: "Doing the Right Thing…"

"They're certainly entitled to think that, and they're
entitled to full respect for their opinions... but before I can
live with other folks I've got to live with myself. The one
thing that doesn't abide by majority rule is a person's
conscience."
~ Harper Lee, "To Kill a Mockingbird"[32]

Justice is the virtue of fairness. It is the first virtue identified by
the Greek philosophers.

Justice is characterized by care and concern for others, particularly with the poor and dispossessed. You demonstrate the
virtue of justice by being fair and kind. Justice is the "golden mean"
between corruption and unfairness. In the Four Virtuous Norms,
Justice fulfills: "Doing the right thing."

The 10 Core Virtues		
Deficit (vice)	**Virtue ("Golden Mean")**	**Excess (vice)**
The Moral Virtues		
Corruption	**1. Justice**	Unfairness
Insensibility	**2. Temperance**	Self-indulgence, Gluttony
Foolishness	**3. Prudence**	Over-cautious
Cowardice	**4. Courage**	Rashness

Justice is the concept of moral rightness and fairness based
on ethics, laws, religion, and so on. As the primary virtue of social
institutions, justice is necessary for society to function. Without
justice, society deteriorates into greed, corruption, oligarchy and
chaos.

Dr. Malloch stated, "Aristotle's notion of justice is also
grounded in a disposition that is entirely internal to the person...
By learning to preside over the internal conflicts of personality
and desire, one becomes just, and so develops abilities to lead in
society as well."[15]

Rosedale High

In the Fall Semester of 1969, I was in my senior year at Delta State, preparing to do my student teaching. When the Dean of the School of Education summoned me to his office, I was apprehensive about what trouble I might be in. One thing for sure, it was going to be either really good or really bad news. He closed the door, and told me that he had an "opportunity" for me. The opportunity was to do my student teaching at Rosedale High School, not far from Delta State in the Mississippi Delta. Rosedale High in 1969 was 100% African-American, faculty and students. (I am not.) Keep in mind this was just months after Dr. King's assassination in Memphis, just 100 miles away, and most schools in Mississippi were still fully segregated.

I accepted the "opportunity". It turned out to be one of the greatest blessings of my life. Yes, there were some tense moments. As most student teachers do, I fell in love with my students and felt their love in return. I learned a powerful lesson about justice that has held me in good stead for over four decades. That lesson is that fairness means all people are not only created equal, but entitled to the same rights regardless of race, creed, color or social status.

Plato treated justice as an all-encompassing virtue of both individuals and societies, meaning that almost every issue he regarded as ethical comes under the notion of justice. Justice seeks to protect the poor from exploitation by the rich. Benevolence is the highest human motive and is in harmony with true justice.

One context to view justice as a virtue is to look at its vices. If you seek more than your "fair share" of goods, you demonstrate the vice of greediness. A just person is one who takes no more than what she merits, her "fair share" of things. Justice does not mean there should be an equitable distribution of goods within a society, but that no one should take more than that which they have earned or have rights to possess, nor should those who cannot provide a basic minimum for themselves and their families go wanting.

D. Joseph Jacques said, "The truth is, justice cannot be found in any judicial system. To find it, we need to look elsewhere. Justice is a moral value that either exists in people, or it does not exist at all."[10] That means justice combines acting justly to the inner ethics of the person rather than simply following the laws or rules. Only when reason governs passion and ambition is your soul harmonious, healthy and strong. Actions are just if they are in agreement with such harmony.

Fairness

Justice emerges from the principles of equality of liberty and opportunity, which ultimately work to the advantage of all. This is what the Founding Fathers called "justice for all"; a fundamental tenet of American democracy. Each person has an equal right to the most extensive total system of equal basic liberties.

Fairness means the cards are not stacked against the poor and in favor of the rich. Everyone plays by the same set of rules. Those who succeed are entitled to the rewards of their efforts, but justice demands that the rich do not have the right to exploit the poor.

In the Six Pillars of Character[11] in "Character Counts" by the Josephson Institute of Ethics teach children the elements of fairness:

- Play by the rules
- Take turns and share
- Be open-minded; listen to others
- Do not take advantage of others
- Do not blame others carelessly
- Treat all people fairly

Aristotle concluded, "All virtue is summed up in dealing justly."[28]

Temperance: "...in the Right Way..."

"Temperance is simply a disposition
of the mind which binds the passion."
~ Thomas Aquinas[28]

Temperance is the virtue of moderation and restraint. Temperance is characterized by self-denial, chastity, modesty, humility, self-control, forgiveness, mercy, and so on, which involves restraining impulses such as sexual desire, vanity, or anger. Temperance is the "golden mean" between insensibility and self-indulgence or gluttony. In the Four Virtuous Norms, temperance fulfills: "Doing the right thing...in the right way".

The 10 Core Virtues		
Deficit (vice)	Virtue ("Golden Mean")	Excess (vice)
The Moral Virtues		
Corruption	1. Justice	Unfairness, oligarchy
Insensibility	2. Temperance	Self-indulgence, Gluttony
Foolishness	3. Prudence	Over-cautious
Cowardice	4. Courage	Rashness

Temperance is moderation in thoughts, actions, and emotions. Considered a core virtue, no other virtue exists without self-control. Temperance is soundness of mind, moderation, discretion. It is the golden mean with regards to pleasures. Pleasures can be divided into those of the soul and the body. Pleasures of the soul include pride, vanity, arrogance, and so on. Bodily pleasures encompass the senses. Not all bodily pleasures are vices, such as delighting in beauty, music or tastes.

The temperate person controls pleasure impulses. For instance, in regards to eating, there are excesses of both gluttony and eating disorders, such as bulimia or anorexia. A temperate person eats neither too much nor too little.

Temperance involves delayed gratification, commonly associated with maturity. Immature children throw temper tantrums when they do not get instant gratification. For instance, imagine a delicious pile of French fries next to a low-fat green salad. If you do not resist the urge to eat the fries, will you then decide to go to the gym for exercise, or succumb to the urge to watch TV? According to a study at Northwestern University, participants who focused on long-term goals were more likely to resist unhealthy urges. When they looked to the future and linked the health task to long-term goals, they exerted self-control and were not affected by being tired or depleted.[27] Temperance is the ability to deny yourself immediate gratification for the good of reaching a long-term goal and all the benefits reaching the goal will bring.

Dr. Malloch said, "The Greeks saw virtues as a unity. Each of the four cardinal virtues depends upon and amplifies the others. A courageous person must be temperate if he is not to overstep the mark. Intemperate courage is not courage but rashness, and temperance in turn needs courage if it is to show its proper worth – the courage to face up to temptation and to the pressure of one's peers and still say no."[15]

Prudence: "…at the Right Time…"

"Hear the words of prudence, give heed unto her counsels, and store them in thine heart; her maxims are universal, and all the virtues lean upon her; she is the guide and the mistress of human life."
~ Akhenaton[25] (Pharaoh of Egypt, 1300s B.C.)

Prudence is the virtue of wisdom and common sense, which implies the ability to see ahead, and means the ability to manage and discipline yourself by the use of reason. Prudence is characterized by being careful about your choices, not taking undue risks and knowing when to act, and when not to act. Prudence is the "golden mean" between foolishness and being overly cautious. In the Four Virtuous Norms, prudence fulfills: "Doing the right thing… at the right time".

| | The 10 Core Virtues | |
Deficit (vice)	Virtue ("Golden Mean")	Excess (vice)
	The Moral Virtues	
Corruption	**1. Justice**	Unfairness, oligarchy
Insensibility	**2. Temperance**	Self-indulgence, Gluttony
Foolishness	**3. Prudence**	Over-cautious
Cowardice	**4. Courage**	Rashness

Wisdom

Prudence includes wisdom, perception, and knowledge. This virtue is the ability to determine the appropriate actions at a given time and place. The Greek philosophers believed the lack of wisdom results in making inappropriate choices instead of prudent ones. Accordingly, wisdom is an asset that impacts the exercise of other virtues. For instance, determining when to act with courage, as opposed to being reckless or cowardly (the vices of courage) is a virtue of prudence. While caution is certainly a part of prudence, over cautiousness can become the vice of cowardice.

My parents' wisdom

My father only went to school through the eighth grade. That was all the education available to him in Calhoun County, Mississippi, in 1915 when he "graduated" from the one-room school. My mother made it through the eleventh grade before she left the poverty of the Mississippi Delta to start a better life. She later completed her education, and became a teacher. My parents both had wisdom, not degrees hanging on the wall, but good old fashioned common sense. Their wisdom came from the "University of Hard Knocks".

I saw my father count using his fingers, but he sold over a million dollars' worth of automobiles in his lifetime. That included the time when new cars sold for hundreds of dollars, not tens of thousands. My mother instilled in all seven of her children that getting a good education was not an option, but a requirement for being a part of our family. My parents embodied all the virtues leading to wisdom and were able to impart that to their children.

What made my parents wise was that they had established their values and principles. The things that were important to them were not the things the world sees as success. Their values were faith, family, and hope. Faith was the core of their being. My father loved to sing hymns that expressed his faith. Family was his pride and joy. He often told us, "I may not have a plug nickel, but I have a million dollar family". In doing so, he pronounced a blessing upon us that many children today never receive from their parents.

Mother instilled hope in each of us that we could become whatever we set our minds to be. Her value of knowledge and virtue of hope for a better life was a blessing that inspired us all.

Common Sense

Prudence is also "practical wisdom", what many today call "common sense". But common sense is not so common. The story of King Solomon's wisdom in treating the two mothers who claimed the same child is an extraordinary example of wisdom.

Prudence involves judgments where the situation must be weighed to determine the appropriate action. Prudent people have the following:

- The ability to withstand self-defeating impulses.
- The ability to focus upon long-term goals and the future, rather than the present.
- The ability to be reflective, deliberate, and realistic about daily life choices.
- The ability to harmonize the goals and interests that motivate them into a firm, coherent, and ethical-conflict free lifestyle.

Courage: "...for the Right Reason"

"Courage is the most important of the virtues, because
without courage you can't practice any other virtue
consistently. You can practice any virtue erratically, but
nothing consistently without courage."
~ Maya Angelou[28]

Courage is the virtue of bravery. Courage implies fortitude,
boldness, and fearlessness. Courage is characterized by the
ability to confront fear, pain, danger, uncertainty, or intimidation
regardless of the circumstances. Courage is the "golden mean"
between cowardice and rashness. In the Four Virtuous Norms,
Courage fulfills "Doing the right thing...for the right reason".

"The 10 Core Virtues"		
Deficit (vice)	Virtue ("Golden Mean")	Excess (vice)
The Moral Virtues		
Corruption	1. Justice	Unfairness, oligarchy
Insensibility	2. Temperance	Self-indulgence, Gluttony
Foolishness	3. Prudence	Over-cautious
Cowardice	4. Courage	Rashness

Ernest Hemingway defined courage when he said, "By 'guts' I
mean, grace under pressure."[28] Bravery is what most people asso-
ciate with courage. Bravery is the ability to stand up for what is
right in spite of the consequences.

Courage is the "golden mean" between its vices of cowardice and fear, or recklessness and over-confidence. We should
note there are times to be fearful. Fear is a normal and beneficial human emotion that alerts us to dangers. Courage is doing
what is right in spite of fear. The courageous person overcomes
fear through rational confidence. Courage involves both physical
courage, such as a soldier headed into battle, and moral courage,

the ability to act rightly in the face of popular opinion. Physical courage involves acting in spite of potential physical harm. Moral courage involves acting for the good in spite of disapproval and criticism.

Sunday visitors

As a minister in the Deep South in the 1980s, long after most schools, restaurants, and society in general had desegregated, the churches remained primarily as they were decades before. Someone said the most segregated hour in America was 11:00 a.m. Sunday.

Serving a church near a college, I came to know many students from diverse ethnic groups as I led lunchtime Bible study groups on campus. Three African American students asked if they could come hear me preach. That was quite a compliment. Of course, I said, "Yes!"

The next Sunday, shortly before worship was to begin, my laity leaders confronted me and asked to meet in my office. "Is there a problem?" I asked. They said there were three black people in the congregation, and gave me the ultimatum to ask them to leave. I responded, "You may have my resignation right now on the spot, but I'm not asking these folks to leave because of the color of their skin." Knowing those students were there to hear my sermon, and not "stir up trouble", I proceeded to the pulpit and began the worship.

Two prominent families got up and walked out of the sanctuary, never to return. I remained at that church for a year longer before moving to my next congregation and ultimately to a new denomination. It took courage, and the church attendance and financial support suffered somewhat, but my character remained intact.

To attain the virtue of courage, Abraham Maslow's "Hierarchy of Needs" offers a model.[31] Maslow expressed human needs on a scale ranging from basic, fundamental physiological needs (including air, water, food) to self-actualization; the ability to act independently of base needs. Maslow held that few achieve self-actualization, mostly because a person must work up the chain of needs. Many people stop at the "belonging" level.

An example of a person who achieved self-actualization was Abraham Lincoln. His decisions to end slavery and conduct an unpopular war were quite controversial. Lincoln was able to do the right things in spite of harsh criticism and threats. Few would argue that Abraham Lincoln possessed and demonstrated the virtue of courage.

A more modern context of courage involves things such as overcoming addictive habits, irrational anxieties, and negative co-dependent relationships. Courage includes perseverance, continuing to seek a goal in the midst of opposition, obstacles, discouragement and even failure. In order to persist at a task, you must be able to suppress the desire to give up and follow an easier task.

Dr. Theodore Malloch wrote, "Virtues are seen at their most admirable in adversity, when they seal the fate of the one who has them. We know this from the virtue of courage. It is certain that the courageous person is more likely to succeed in life, since he will take the risks on which success depends. But it is also certain that in real adversity he is more at risk than the coward. Like the Spartans of Thermopylae, the courageous person will stand firm in the line of duty until cut down. This doesn't show courage to be irrational. On the contrary, it shows that the virtue we need to conduct ordinary life may, in extraordinary circumstances, expose us to danger. But the same virtue will, in those circumstances, bring admiration, too, and the honor and praise that is the hero's due."[15]

The U.S. Navy devotes a section to Courage in its Core Values:

COURAGE

Courage is the value that gives me the moral and mental strength to do what is right, with confidence and resolution, even in the face of temptation or adversity.

I will:

- Have the courage to meet the demands of my profession and the mission entrusted to me.
- Make decisions and act in the best interest of the Department of the Navy and the nation, without regard to personal consequences.

- Overcome all challenges while adhering to the highest standards of personal conduct and decency.
- Be loyal to my nation by ensuring the resources entrusted to me are used in an honest, careful and efficient way.

Chapter 6

Your Noble Virtues

"I long to accomplish a great and noble task,
but it is my chief duty to accomplish small tasks
as if they were great and noble."
~ Helen Keller[25]

"The ABC Model" organizes "The 10 Core Virtues" into three groupings: Moral, Noble, and Spiritual Virtues. The noble virtues are honesty, trust, and discipline.

Some philosophers identify these as "ethical virtues". Since "The ABC Model" identifies ethics and virtues apart from each other, the term "ethical virtues" in this context is confusing. That is not to say they do not relate. To prevent confusion, we identify the virtues of honesty, trust and discipline as noble virtues.

MORAL VIRTUES	NOBLE VIRTUES	SPIRITUAL VIRTUES
Justice	**Honesty**	Faith
Temperance	**Trust**	Hope
Prudence	**Discipline**	Love
Courage		

The Merriam-Webster Dictionary[26] defines noble as "possessing very high or excellent qualities or properties, and possessing, characterized by, or arising from superiority of mind or character or of ideals or morals". As with all virtues, they emerge from the soul. To exemplify these virtues requires human willpower.

Aristotle argued "the good life" is a life consisting of noble actions. The noble virtues of honesty, trust and discipline are the most tangible of all the virtues. They are the ones most commonly seen and experienced by others. Cicero said "Nothing is nobler, nothing more venerable than fidelity. Faithfulness and truth are the most sacred excellences and endowments of the human mind."[28]

In this chapter, we examine the nature of these three principal virtues.

Honesty: Your Whole Truth

"If you tell the truth you don't have
to remember anything."
~ Mark Twain[25]

Honesty is the virtue of truthfulness. Honesty is the virtue most commonly associated with integrity. An honest person is one who speaks the truth, practices honest dealings, or does not cheat. Honesty is the "golden mean" between the vices of dishonesty or lying and boastfulness.

The 10 Core Virtues		
Deficit (vice)	Virtue ("Golden Mean")	Excess (vice)
The Noble Virtues		
Dishonesty	**5. Honesty**	Boastfulness
Suspicion, Distrust	**6. Trust**	Gullible, Blind Trust
Sloth, Apathy	**7. Discipline**	Obsession, Compulsion

When asked, "What is integrity?" most people respond with honesty. While honesty is one of the most important components of integrity, honesty is not equal to integrity. Honesty is a virtue, similar to trust, courage and justice. A person of integrity will be a person of honesty, but an honest person is not always a person of integrity.

To sign or not to sign
I was forty years old when I ended the career I had worked all my life to build. As pastor of a large church, my career was progressing nicely. There were power struggles and back room politics at the top of the denomination that were down right un-Christian. I witnessed many character assassinations that ended brilliant careers, especially among my former seminary professors, who received the Scarlet Letter "L" (for being too "liberal").

It would have been easy to look the other way, to say it does not concern me. In my heart, I knew I could no longer support the leadership who kept a Nixon-style "friends lists", blacklisting anyone who dared challenge their authority. The final straw came when they demanded all pastors sign a pledge that they believed "God created the heaven and earth in seven literal 24-hour days". Otherwise, our names would go on the list, and we would never be considered for any of the "plum pulpits" in that area. I'm still wondering how they knew the first three days were "literal 24-hours" long since the Bible says the sun, moon and stars were not created until the fourth day. Who was holding the stopwatch? And how was she able to see it in the dark?

To sign or not to sign: That was the question. Ironically the national meeting of that denomination was in San Antonio that year. I remember standing outside the Alamo, contemplating the courage and bravery of those men who died defending their freedom. That is when I decided to do the unthinkable. I resigned my pulpit in protest, left that denomination, and faced a highly uncertain future. It was one of the most courageous things I have ever done, and God has blessed me since beyond measure.

Aristotle described two kinds of vices of truth, one who over-states things, which he called boastfulness, and one who under-states things, a false modesty. An honest person does not tell the truth once, but habitually.

What is honesty?

We define honesty as the quality of being truthful and sincere; devoid of deceit.

Ask someone to define honesty and most likely the responses will be:

- Honesty is telling the truth.
- Honesty is forthright conduct.
- Honesty is being genuine, truthful, trustworthy, honorable, fair, and loyal.
- Honesty is doing the right thing, even when no one is looking.

Is honesty the best policy?

General Robert E. Lee qualified the adage: "The trite saying that honesty is the best policy has met with the just criticism that honesty is not policy. The real honest man is honest from conviction of what is right, not from policy."[28]

The Whole Truth

To testify in court, a witness takes a sworn oath to "tell the truth, the whole truth, and nothing but the truth." Honesty and truth relate closely, although you may analyze each apart from one another. An honest person tells the truth. But truth does not equate to honesty, as that truth may be simply factual, whereas honesty is a character trait or virtue. Plus, the virtue of honesty precludes withholding information that gives an incomplete and dishonest account.

Likewise, an honest person is not one who simply conducts honest business, or does not cheat. Doing such actions from fear of being caught, rather than the motive "to do otherwise would be dishonest", are not the actions of an honest person.

The motives with respect to honest and dishonest actions reflect your views about honesty and truth. The lover of truth is truthful, even when nothing depends on it.

George Washington held many distinguished titles. However, he said, "I hope I shall possess firmness and virtue enough to maintain what I consider the most enviable of all titles, the character of an honest man."[25] Deepak Chopra warns, "Walk with those seeking truth... RUN FROM THOSE WHO THINK THEY'VE FOUND IT."[2]

Trust: Keeping Your Word

"The best way to find out if you can trust
somebody is to trust them."
~ Ernest Hemingway[28]

Trust is the virtue of fidelity, loyalty and confidence. Trust is characterized by the person who demonstrates reliability, dependability, consistency, loyalty, trustworthiness and earned confidence. Trust is the "golden mean" between distrust or suspicion and blind trust or gullibility.

The 10 Core Virtues		
Deficit (vice)	Virtue ("Golden Mean")	Excess (vice)
The Noble Virtues		
Dishonesty	5. Honesty	Boastfulness
Suspicion, Distrust	6. Trust	Gullible, Blind Trust
Sloth, Apathy	7. Discipline	Obsession, Compulsion

Of all the virtues, trust may be the most difficult to conceptualize. We easily conjure up images of love, courage, discipline, and so on. But what does trust look like? Sure, you know it when we see it; or more accurately, when you experience it. Trust is an essential foundation of integrity. It is as indispensable as anything you, your business or organization possesses. With trust, you will succeed. Without trust, failure is inevitable.

Cancer

No one wants to hear the "C" word. I heard it May 15, 2008. Prostate cancer! I feared I would die before surgery and radiation could be completed. I confess my faith wavered as I confronted what may be my greatest battle. Today, I am one of millions of cancer survivors who are in remission, leading relatively normal, productive lives. What cancer taught me was to trust: trust the

Great Physician, trust life, trust my doctors, and yes, even trust eternity.

The Speed of Trust

Stephen M. R. Covey[5], son of Stephen Covey, along with Rebecca R. Merrill[17] wrote in their book, *The Speed of Trust: The One Thing That Changes Everything*: "There is one thing that is common to every individual, relationship, team, family, organization, nation, economy, and civilization throughout the world – one thing which, if removed, will destroy the most powerful government, the most successful business, the most thriving economy, the most influential leadership, the greatest friendship, the strongest character, the deepest love. On the other hand, if developed and leveraged, that one thing has the potential to create unparalleled success and prosperity in every dimension of life. Yet, it is the least understood, most neglected, and most underestimated possibility of our time. That one thing is trust." [5]

Covey challenges the notion that trust is a passive social virtue. Instead, he shows that trust is a learnable and measurable ability that makes people more successful, relationships more stimulating, and organizations more profitable. "Simply put, trust means confidence. The opposite of trust – distrust - is suspicion. When you trust people, you have confidence in them - in their integrity and in their abilities. When you distrust people, you are suspicious of them - of their integrity, their agenda, their capabilities, or their track record. It's that simple. We have all had experiences that validated the difference between relationships that are built on trust and those that are not. These experiences clearly tell us the difference is not small; it is dramatic." [5]

There are two sides to trust: being a person who can be trusted, and being a person who trusts others. Trust is being trustworthy, dependable, and consistent. A trustworthy person is someone in whom you can place your trust and rest assured that the trust will not be betrayed or disappointed. A trustworthy person is someone who is dependable, who keeps both their promises and confidences. A trustworthy person is someone who is consistent; whose behavior does not surprise you with mixed episodes of trust and disappointment. Earning trust requires your trust must be proven over time.

Trust is crucial because it allows you to form relationships and depend on others for everything from love, advice, to household repairs. Trust is the first quality a person demands in a relationship. You put trust in all sorts of people and things every day; the airplane pilot, the doctor, the mail carrier, the restaurant chef, your wristwatch, your car's brakes, and so on. Trust involves the risk that the person or thing trusted will not prove trustworthy. If there were some guarantee, then there would be no need to trust. Therefore, trust is also dangerous. Trust is necessary for society, because an atmosphere of virtues enhance trustworthiness. In a democratic society, people may trust one another more than in a totalitarian or corrupt society.

How to become a person of trust
The characteristics of the trust virtue relate to your overall ethics, virtues, character and integrity. In other words, the process to establish, earn and maintain trust is to build character that exemplifies trust. That is to say virtues complement, validate and strengthen each other. For instance, by being honest, you strengthen your virtue of trust. By demonstrating temperance, prudence, courage and justice, you make yourself a more trustworthy person in the eyes of your family, friends and peers.

Becoming a person of trust begins with trusting yourself. Believe that you can and will be a trustworthy person in your personal, family and professional relationships.

Form trust relationships. By becoming a person of trust, you will find trustworthy people with whom you may form trusting bonds. These mutually beneficial trust relationships become increasingly significant in your personal and professional life. Ranging from someone you trust to share a frustration or bounce an idea off, to executing an agreement worth millions of dollars, your trust partners will enhance your life, and you will enrich their lives. Do not be surprised when a former colleague recommends you to her new company, because she knows you are a person of trust.

Work at your trust. It requires a high level of effort to build and maintain trust. Trust, like your reputation, is one of your most valuable assets. You cannot afford to lose it. So cherish and nurture your personal trust and trust relationships.

The good news is that as you build trust, it becomes a habit, or second nature. You will find that doing something distrustful becomes repugnant to you; something alien to your character.

The benefits of trust

The value of trust is hard to overestimate. Trust is at the basis of morality. A moral society bases itself upon trusting one another to at least try to be moral. Trust is the basis for commerce and business. High-trust societies have stronger economies and social capital than low-trust societies. Managers who micromanage do not trust their employees, and ultimately limit the potential of their organization by failing to provide leadership.

Trust is the basis of society. Trust begins in infancy, where babies learn to trust their parents for their basic needs and love. Unfortunately, children must learn the hard lesson of distrust for their own safety. Trusting others to honor their social promises and commitments makes human bonds possible. Even if trust does not make society possible, it makes it healthier and stronger.

Trust lost and regained

How can trust be restored once it is lost? Destroying trust can happen quickly and startlingly easily. Recreating trust is a slow and painful process. What if you trusted your life savings to Bernie Madoff? What if your spouse was unfaithful? What if your business partner is stealing from your company? What if the police arrest your teenage daughter for texting while driving that caused an auto accident? Would there be anything they could do to reestablish your trust? Each of these situations illustrates how difficult, but maybe not impossible, it is to reestablish trust once lost.

It is vital to note that transgressions of your integrity are the most difficult to reestablish, if at all. Slips of the tongue, a moment of poor judgment are different from betrayal or felony.

While the subject is extremely complex and circumstantial, here are some principles to guide if and (heaven forbid) when you break your bond of trust.

1. Admit your failing. Cover-ups and lying make things 100 times worse.
2. Apologize. Confession is good for the soul.
3. Ask for forgiveness. You may not get it, but you must ask.

4. Accept the responsibility. Do not blame others. Remember that words are cheap.
5. Make restitution. As much as possible, mend what you broke.
6. Realize what you do not control. You cannot make people trust you again.
7. Realize what you do control. You alone control your trust-worthiness from today forward.

"Trust me!" Trust is a choice. Trust can still be cultivated.

The Six Pillars of Character[11] of "Character Counts" by Josephson Institute of Ethics teach children trustworthiness, including:

- Be honest.
- Do not deceive, cheat, or steal.
- Be reliable — do what you say you will do.
- Have the courage to do the right thing.
- Build a good reputation.
- Be loyal — stand by your family, friends, and country.

Discipline: Your Self-Control

"The only discipline that lasts is self-discipline."
~ Bum Phillips[28]

Discipline is the virtue of self-control and patience. Discipline is characterized by the person who demonstrates self-control. Discipline is the "golden mean" between slothfulness or apathy and compulsion or obsession.

The 10 Core Virtues		
Deficit (vice)	**Virtue ("Golden Mean")**	**Excess (vice)**
The Noble Virtues		
Dishonesty	**5. Honesty**	Boastfulness
Suspicion, Distrust	**6. Trust**	Gullible, Blind Trust
Sloth, apathy	**7. Discipline**	Obsession, Compulsion

Discipline is the virtue of control over your mind, body, passions and actions. In that sense, it holds much in common with other virtues, especially prudence and temperance. In its basic meaning, discipline is the systematic instruction given to disciples to study in a skill, craft, occupation or activity in which they will perform, or follow a code, profession or order. A disciple is one who seeks to develop into the character-likeness of the teacher or coach.

Discipline means a person has mastery over one or more trait; such as speech. A person with this discipline knows what to say (or not say), when to say it, and what words to use (prudent and positive words instead of vile and angry words). Likewise, an athlete disciplines the body so that the race may be won, and the soldier disciplines for battle.

Money

I wish the reason I wrote this book was because I am the epitome of integrity. I am far from it, just ask my wife. I wrote this book because I have learned from many mistakes. Some are quite significant, and I want to share that if I can do it, there is hope for anyone who has messed up.

While I am not about to make public confession of all my sins, I honestly share handling finances was a colossal failing in my earlier life. It was not that my parents had not taught me better. It was not that I did not make enough money. But as the proverb puts it, "If your outgo exceeds your income, your upkeep will become your downfall."

If every other area of my life was perfect, lack of discipline in handling money was destroying any chance I had to achieve integrity or happiness. I had dug myself a pretty deep hole. Thanks to my wife and the teachings of Dave Ramsey, the popular financial advisor, I began, slowly but surely, to get my financial house in order. It required much discipline, and years of hard work. Persistence paid off. I am now fully debt free, and learned how to save money. If I can do it, anyone can.

Self-discipline

Discipline expresses itself as self-discipline. For that matter, all virtues are "self" virtues.

In *The Road Less Traveled*, Dr. M. Scott Peck[21] described four aspects of discipline:

- Delaying gratification: Sacrificing present comfort for future gains.
- Acceptance of responsibility: Accepting responsibility for one's own decisions.
- Dedication to truth: Honesty, both in word and deed.
- Balancing: Handling conflicting requirements. Scott Peck talks of "bracketing", an important skill to prioritize between different requirements.

Self-discipline means purposely aligning your energy with your values and ideals. You focus on the task before you, the goal you strive to achieve, and ignore other distractions and temptations. Self-discipline asks that you endure temptations and distractions in the pursuit of a higher goal. It means being willing to push yourself to the limits of your determination and perseverance. Self-discipline may take the form of a quiet commitment or determination that then directs your choices. Self-discipline enables you to be all that you can be in the pursuit of your dreams.

Discipline asserts willpower over sensual desires. Self-discipline is comparable to motivation, when you use reason to determine the best course of action that opposes your desires. Virtuous, disciplined behavior is when motivations align with your reasoned ideals and goals: to do what is best, and to do it with excellence.

Self-control is the ability to control your emotions, behavior, and desires in order to achieve some reward, or avoid some punishment. Self-control connects with useful life results, such as happiness. Self-discipline can be defined as the ability to motivate yourself in spite of a negative feelings. Qualities associated with self-discipline include willpower, hard work, and persistence. Self-discipline is the result of sustained willpower. Whereas willpower is the strength and ability to carry out a specific task, self-discipline is the ability to use it regularly and even spontaneously (as a habit).[31]

Patience (or forbearing) is determination under difficult circumstances, which means persevering in the face of obstacles without giving up. Patience is the amount of adversity you can endure. It refers to the character trait of being steadfast. Antonyms include hastiness and impetuousness.

Patience appears in The Books of Wisdom in the Bible:

- "A patient man has great understanding, but a quick-tempered man displays folly." (Proverbs 14:29 NIV).
- "A hot-tempered man stirs up dissension, but a patient man calms a quarrel." (Proverbs 15:18 NIV).
- "Better a patient man than a warrior, a man who controls his temper than one who takes a city."
  (Proverbs 16:32 NIV).
- "Patience is better than pride. Do not be quickly provoked in your spirit, for anger resides in the lap of fools."
  (Ecclesiastes 7:8-9 NIV).

In Christianity, patience is one of the most useful virtues of life. While patience is not one of the traditional three spiritual virtues, nor one of the four traditional cardinal virtues, patience and self-control are parts of the "Fruits of the Spirit" found in Galatians 5:21-23:

1. Love
2. Joy
3. Peace
4. **Patience**
5. Kindness
6. Goodness
7. Faithfulness
8. Gentleness
9. **Self-control**

"Against such things there is no law".

Chapter 7

Your Spiritual Virtues

"We are not human beings on a spiritual journey.
We are spiritual beings on a human journey."
~ Stephen R. Covey[28]

The last grouping of "The 10 Core Virtues" are The Spiritual Virtues; faith, hope and charity (or love, agape). While many express these virtues in religious terms, especially in Christianity, they are essential elements of religious, spiritual and secular life.

MORAL VIRTUES	NOBLE VIRTUES	SPIRITUAL VIRTUES
Justice	Honesty	**Faith**
Temperance	Trust	**Hope**
Prudence	Discipline	**Charity (Love, agape)**
Courage		

The Greek philosophers debated whether virtues such as faith, hope, and love, are logical, rational premises, which makes them ethics rather than virtues; or are they ethics in action, qualifying them as virtues. "The ABC Model" reinforces the traditional position that faith, hope and charity are certainly virtues; things we do rather than things we surmise.

Likewise, faith, hope and non-romantic love are not merely emotions. As virtues, they spring from within your will, not your emotions. That is not to say never are emotions involved, especially as with love. It is to say do not confuse the emotions associated with these virtues with the virtue itself.

Deepak Chopra, in *War of the Worldviews, Science vs. Spirituality*, argues that religion is not the same as spirituality.[2] For Dr. Chopra, spirituality is deeper than religion, which he argues sometimes gets in the way of spirituality. His challenger, Dr. Leonard Mlodinow, conceded that while scientists "seek to ensure their measurements and concepts are not influenced by 'love, trust, faith, beauty awe, wonder, compassion' etc., does not mean they dismiss the values of those qualities in other areas of life".[18]

Chopra and Mlodinow agree there are unquestionably spiritual components to human life, whether you are highly religious or an avowed atheist. Assuming you are a spiritual being (but not necessarily religious), it behooves you to assess your intrinsic spiritual virtues.

Your spiritual awareness itself inspires you to be virtuous. The more you understand your spiritual nature, the more sense it makes for you to act with honesty, compassion, and humility. See how one virtue leads to another. Spiritual virtues manifest themselves naturally through the way you think and the things you do. When you see life with spiritual awareness, virtuous actions are the only behavior that makes sense. That leads to spiritual integrity, where body, soul and spirit are one and whole with actions, beliefs and character.

Dr. M. Scott Peck[21] suggests that there are four stages of human spiritual development:

Stage I is Chaos. It is similar to small children, prone to tantrums, rebellion and must get their own way. They are extremely selfish. Some people never grow out of Stage I, especially criminals.

Stage II is Fundamentalism. It sees the world divided into good and evil, we and they, right or wrong. Many religious people are at Stage II; they have "blind faith". They show humility and a willingness to obey and serve. Many good, decent people never move past Stage II.

Stage III is Skepticism. It is the stage of questioning. These are the people who do not accept things on faith. Many reject the existence of the spiritual or supernatural. Some retain their religious principles, but move beyond the fundamental rigid doctrines.

Stage IV is Maturity. It is the stage of accepting the mystery and beauty of nature and existence. While skeptical, these people develop a deeper understanding of good and evil, forgiveness and mercy, compassion and love. They have a faith based upon genuine belief. According to Peck, this is the stage of loving others as yourself, losing your attachment to your ego, and forgiving your enemies.

Theodore Roosevelt Malloch[15] is Chairman and CEO of The Roosevelt Group, is a research professor at Yale University, where he founded the Spiritual Capital Initiative and produced the documentary, Doing Virtuous Business. The film explores the concept of "values-based" management strategies that can both improve the bottom line and strengthen a company's relationships with customers, employees, vendors, the environment, and the world at large.

Dr. Malloch addressed the question, "Can the concept of "Spiritual Capital" actually ensure a company's success?"[15] Drawing from the notion of "social capital," developed by generations of scholars, Malloch adds the concept of "spiritual capital" as a basis for social progress and also a necessity for responsible and profitable enterprise. He details the virtues that maintain a business and free market-virtues that make up a network of trust, which is essential to the global economy.

Malloch reveals that a company's soul determines its "spiritual capital," an equally indispensable foundation to success. From Wal-Mart to IBM, Malloch demonstrates how companies that operate on ethical models informed by spiritual traditions have outperformed their competitors. Besides making the world a better place, Malloch argues virtuous enterprise makes companies far more successful and profitable than they otherwise would be. He presents case studies of virtuous business in the Judeo-Christian tradition as well as statistical analysis demonstrating how companies that operate on ethical models have outperformed their competitors over the long run.[15]

Faith: Your Beliefs in Action

"Faith is a knowledge within the heart, beyond the reach of proof."
~ Khalil Gibran[28]

Faith is the virtue of assurance and confidence. Faith is characterized by the person who demonstrates faithfulness, fidelity, loyalty, confidence, and belief. Faith is the "golden mean" between doubt or anxiety and blind faith or over-confidence.

The 10 Core Virtues		
Deficit (vice)	Virtue ("Golden Mean")	Excess (vice)
The Spiritual Virtues		
Doubt, Anxiety	**8. Faith**	Blind Faith, Over-confidence
Despair, Cynicism	**9. Hope**	Presumption, False Hope
Indifference, Ingratitude	**10. Charity (agape)**	Greed, Wastefulness

The word faith translates from the Greek as believe. Faith differs from beliefs in that beliefs are internal, rational premises (ethical), and faith is an act of goodness (virtue). This illustrates the connection between beliefs and faith, because your faith emerges from your beliefs. However, you must take care to distinguish your faith and beliefs. In this context, it would be incorrect to say "My beliefs are my faith". Faith is your beliefs in action.

Hebrews 11:1 defines faith as, "the assurance of things hoped for, the evidence of things not seen". Paul writes in Ephesians 2:8-9, "For by grace are ye saved through faith; and that not of yourselves: it is the gift of God: Not of works, lest any man should boast."

Stepping out on faith

Rarely have I made appeals for money from the pulpit, but things were getting so bad at the church, I had to ask the congregation to dig a bit deeper into their pocketbooks. One of the most humbling experiences of my ministry was when I received a call from a single mother the following week, who said, "It worked!" I asked "What worked?" She had responded to my appeal by placing the last money she had in the offering plate. That meant she and her daughter had no money for food, gasoline, or anything until her next paycheck, which was over a week away. Before I could say anything, she said a large, unexpected check arrived in the mail. It was, she explained, a blessing for her stepping out in faith to help her church.

I was extremely fortunate to know Dr. Wayne Oates, my professor of pastoral care and counseling in seminary, who coined the word "workaholic". We became friends, and kept in touch for many years after I graduated. Dr. Oates' cross-disciplinary approach earned him the title "father of the modern pastoral care movement". In his book, *Anxiety in Christian Experience*, Dr. Oates stated, "The opposite of faith is not doubt, but anxiety."[19] By that, he meant that without faith, doubts and fears give rise to anxiety and neuroses.

Leonard Mlodinow, theoretical physicist wrote: "None of us can function without having faith of one sort or another. Entrepreneurs start businesses on faith, immigrants with no concrete prospects move to another country on faith, writers toil for long hours in the faith that people will want to read their words."[18] Indeed, great scientists like Dr. Mlodinow place abundant faith in such premises as the Big Bang, quantum physics and evolution.

The virtues of faith, trust and hope relate to each other. Faith grounds hope. Hope grounded in faith is strong enough to overcome periods of pain, sorrow and even tragedy. Likewise, there is a relationship between faith and trust. Faith and trust both involve a venture, in which you surrender some level of control over yourself.

Faith involves the mind, the emotions and the will. In one sense, all your actions are expressions of faith at some level. John Calvin, the Reformer, said faith is "revealed to our minds and sealed upon our hearts". This illustrates faith's connection between your mind and will. Faith provides a sense of trust and confidence necessary for a successful and happy life.

Faith goes beyond reason. It involves accepting what cannot be established as true through the proper exercise of your intellect.

As Emmanuel Kant, the modern philosopher, said, "I have ... found it necessary to deny knowledge, in order to make room for faith". (Stanford Encyclopedia of Philosophy, plato.stanford.edu.)

C.S. Lewis in his book, *Mere Christianity*, describes faith as "the art of holding on to things your reason has once accepted, in spite of your changing moods."[14]

Hope: The Anchor of Your Soul

"Hope is the dream of a waking man."
~ Aristotle

Hope is the virtue of optimism, confidence and assurance. Hope is characterized by the person who demonstrates an unwavering calm assurance that things will work out for the good and overcomes life's trials, troubles and tragedies. Hope is the "golden mean" between despair or cynicism and presumption or false hope.

The 10 Core Virtues		
Deficit (vice)	Virtue ("Golden Mean")	Excess (vice)
The Spiritual Virtues		
Doubt, Anxiety	8. Faith	Blind Faith, Over-confidence
Despair, Cynicism	9. Hope	Presumption, False Hope
Indifference, Ingratitude	10. Charity (agape)	Greed, Wastefulness

Like all virtues, hope is an active exercise of your will rather than just a belief. Stated differently, hope is something you do rather than something you have. That means it is active behavior, not a passive belief. Certainly, after exercising hope, you have hope.

Faith and hope relate to each other and often get confused as being the same. Whereas faith is the putting of beliefs (your ethics) into actions; hope is exercising your will (your soul's anchor) that all things will work together for the good.

The New Testament defines hope as the sure and steadfast "anchor of the soul". "We who have fled to take hold of the hope offered to us may be greatly encouraged. We have this hope as an anchor for the soul, firm and secure." (Hebrews 6:18-19 NIV). Hope is a strong and confident expectation, an essential and fundamental element of spiritual life, along with faith and love. Paul the Apostle wrote, "But hope that is seen is no hope at all. Who hopes for what he already has? But if we hope for what we do not yet have, we wait for it patiently." (Romans 8:24-25 NIV).

Cross country

When my wife's job relocated in San Diego, I came along, all the way from Mississippi. I hoped to get a pastoral appointment, even a small church in the desert that I could drive out to on the weekends.

The District Superintendent thanked me for asking, but kindly informed me this Conference had 450 elders and 400 churches. My chances of getting an appointment were few. So we began attending worship at First United Methodist Church in San Diego. It was a blessing to be on the other side of the pulpit and able to sit with my wife in worship for a change. I never gave up hope of getting an assignment.

Six months went by. One day the phone rang. The District Superintendent asked if I remained interested in receiving an appointment. The church was not in the desert; it was about one mile from where we lived. I served that congregation for twelve years, and continue to serve as their pastor emeritus. Never give up hope!

What is hope?

Hope combines the desire for something and the assumption of receiving it, while at the same time providing a quiet assurance that frees you from anxiety over obtaining it. Without hope, you are like a child on a journey who asks every ten seconds, "Are we there yet?" When you apply hope, calm assurance replaces anxiety as the anchor within your soul. However, hope is more than positive thinking. It is also not mere tenacity, or "clinging to your hopes". Hope provides you with a firm assurance that will sustain you through human tragedies, troubles, and even trials of faith that may otherwise seem overwhelming.

Hope provides a dynamic link between the present and future. It is the act of expectation that brings meaning into what you are doing now with what you envision tomorrow, next year, and thereafter. The things for which you hope guide you. Hope emerges from your ethics, where you formulate ideals and goals for the person you want to become, exercise your determination to achieve those goals, and realize those goals. Take away your hope, and you find yourself in despair and without direction.

Hope allows you to transcend the temporal, daily conditions of life, connecting you to the eternal; the Divine. Hope removes fear and despair, allowing you to become productive and have confidence in a better future. Hopeful people are like the little engine that could, because they keep telling themselves "I think I can, I think I can, I KNOW I can!"

Case Study: "Tired of Hope"

Todd and David are prostate cancer (PC) survivors. So is this author. We all belong to an online PC support group, HealingWell.

Todd had a prostate specific antigen (PSA) level of 3,216 when diagnosed in 2007. Anything over 4.0 gets the doctor's attention. He had stage 4 prostate cancer, meaning it had spread to other parts of his body. He admits his survival is a miracle.

Recently, Todd wrote: "Last night in my dream, I was the speaker before the luminary and I said this. 35 years ago President Carter declared war on cancer. Thirty five years later I walk in my 8th Relay for Life. I am a 7 year stage 4 prostate cancer survivor. When one considers my stats at diagnosis it is quite remarkable that I will walk my eighth luminary lap. I am happy to be here to do it. I am blessed when so many others have not had the same results. What bothers me however is that tonight will be the same as last year and the year before, and the year before. Halfway through the lap tonight the word Hope will turn to Cure. The only difference will be another hundred luminary candles lining the path.

"I am tired of Hope. I am tired of my friends and family dying from this disease. I am tired of cat scans and bone scans. I am tired of treatments that cost tens of thousands for a few months. I am tired of people getting rich off of the pain of others .... I am tired of clinging to hope that for me is month to month. I am tired of looking to the horizon for the next treatment that will give me a few more months.

"When do we move on to CURE! WHEN DO WE SAY ENOUGH? 35 years ago war was declared on cancer not cancer patients. The time for a cure is not tomorrow. The time for a cure is now."

David replied to Todd's posting. In 2008, David's prostate cancer was his fourth cancer diagnosis. His radiation treatment went horribly wrong, and he lives each day in excruciating pain. Plus, his prostate cancer has recurred. David read Todd's comments and wrote his following reply:

"Your subject says "Tired of Hope". I can't say that I would ever agree with that premise, assuming you meant that to be a literal statement. Hope is the only thing that keeps me going most days. The hope that things might reverse with my cancer's growth. Hope that my high climbing and fast moving PSA will either slow down or reverse before any metastasis show up. Hoping I don't have bladder cancer or pancreatic cancer. Hope that I can endure another 24 hours of pain. Hope that my wife and family never give up on me. Hope that I can stay strong enough to keep fighting.

"To me, being "tired of hope", would mean I am giving up on hope, or have become impatient with hope, etc. Not putting words in your mouth, it means for you, whatever you meant when you wrote it. I find in the words of many at HealingWell, that there is a certain amount of fear of death and dying. Perhaps that is human nature at work. Even dying needs to be embraced, it's a natural process in all living things. There is never any fairness in dying, so that rule shouldn't be applied. I find, that by accepting death, and even embracing it, makes it easier to accept.

"I don't hope I will live forever, but I do hope I can die a painless death with dignity. It bothers me when I read things like "we will all beat this thing", etc. We will not all beat death from PC. If we hang around HealingWell long enough, there will be names here that didn't make it. But that shouldn't bother or scare anyone; that is again part of the natural course of events. PC still kills nearly 30,000 men a year in this country alone, despite treatments, courage, and fighting the good fight until the end. Unless a cure is found, this pattern will continue over and over and over again.

"Never give up on hope, the opposite of hope, is hopelessness."

David and Todd are wrestling deep within their souls with hope in the face of menacing circumstances. However, do not overlook the strength their hope brings into their spirits.

Conclusion

In the mythological Greek story of Zeus, Pandora's Box contained all manner of obscure evils released onto the world when someone opened the box. Hope, which lay at the bottom of the box, remained. The story illustrates that your only weapon against the trials and tribulations of this life is hope that things will get better.

If you want and need strength and stability to overcome the trials, tribulations and tragedies of life, you will find it within your soul's anchor; your hope.

"Hope springs eternal."
~ Alexander Pope[28], *Essay on Man*

Love and Charity: Your Greatest Virtue

"Behold I do not give lectures or a little charity, When I
give I give myself."
~ Walt Whitman[28]

Love is the virtue of caring and charity. Love is characterized by the person who demonstrates the concepts and virtues of justice, kindness, spiritual and physical love. It is "the greatest" of the three spiritual virtues. Love is the "golden mean" between indifference and ingratitude and greed or wastefulness.

The 10 Core Virtues		
Deficit (vice)	Virtue ("Golden Mean")	Excess (vice)
The Spiritual Virtues		
Doubt, Anxiety	8. Faith	Blind Faith, Over-confidence
Despair, Cynicism	9. Hope	Presumption, False Hope
Indifference, Ingratitude	10. Charity (agape)	Greed, Wastefulness

What is charity (love, or agape)?

The word Paul used for love in 1 Corinthians 13 is agape in the Greek; commonly translated as charity. Charity involves love of God and love of mankind, which include both love of your neighbor and yourself. Charity is concern for, and active helping of, others. (Who is my brother, my neighbor?) Love, in the sense of loving-kindness towards all others, is the highest perfection of the human spirit.

"If I could speak all the languages of earth and of angels, but didn't love others, I would only be a noisy gong or a clanging cymbal.

If I had the gift of prophecy, and if I understood all of God's secret plans and possessed all knowledge, and if I had such faith that I could move mountains, but didn't love others, I would be nothing.

If I gave everything I have to the poor and even sacrificed my body, I could boast about it; but if I didn't love others, I would have gained nothing.

Love is patient and kind.

Love is not jealous or boastful or proud or rude.

It does not demand its own way.

It is not irritable, and it keeps no record of being wronged.

It does not rejoice about injustice but rejoices whenever the truth wins out.

Love never gives up, never loses faith, is always hopeful, and endures through every circumstance.

Three things will last forever—faith, hope, and love—and the greatest of these is love."

~ 1 Corinthians 13 (New Living Translation)

In his book, *The Road Less Traveled*, Dr. M. Scott Peck wrote that love is not a feeling; it is an activity and an investment. He defines love as, "The will to extend one's self for the purpose of nurturing one's own or another's spiritual growth". Love is primarily actions towards nurturing the spiritual growth of another. It consists of what you do for another person. Peck added, "Love is as love does." It is about giving yourself and the other person what they need to grow.[21]

From Russia with love

In the middle of radiation treatments for cancer, I remember praying one evening that God would show me how to make my church's ministry meaningful. Suddenly, I remembered a young woman pastor from Russia who spoke to the Annual Conference the year before. I recall she spoke through an interpreter, and that her ministry specialized in serving the "street orphans" somewhere in eastern Russia.

About that same time, someone on the television said, "There are places in the world, like Russia, where one U.S. dollar has the purchasing power ten times locally." It was as if the Holy Spirit connected me with her, directing me to give a modest regular offering to help her buy food and clothes for the street orphans. I did not know her name. I did not know where she lived. I certainly do not speak Russian.

The next day, I learned that the Methodist Russian Initiative was underway here in San Diego. Weak from my surgery and radiation, I made my way to the meeting where I met the pastor's District Superintendent who knew exactly who I was talking about. She connected me with Pastor Elena in Khabarovsk, Far East (Siberia), Russia. A few days later, I received an email from her in perfect English. God had transcended the miles, the unknown, and the language barrier to connect us. We began collecting a communion offering every first Sunday of the month. I have been wiring 100% of the funds to Pastor Elena's church ever since, which she uses to feed, clothe, and educate young orphans living on the street.

Love is time

An intriguing concept is that love is time. That means we love what and whom we spend our time. If we say we love someone, but never spend time with them, the profession of love does not seem genuine. We will make time for those people and things we truly love.

Charity

Some describe charity to mean only benevolent giving. The poor, particularly widows and orphans, the sick and disabled, are the proper objects of charity. Most forms of charity focus on providing food, water, clothing, and shelter, and tending the ill, but other actions may be performed as charity: visiting the imprisoned or the homebound and educating orphans.

The Six Pillars of Character[11] in "Character Counts" by Josephson Institute of Ethics teach students love is caring that includes:

- Be kind.
- Be compassionate and show you care.
- Express gratitude.
- Forgive others.
- Help people in need.

Section Three

Character: Why You Do It

"Character is that which reveals moral purpose,
exposing the class of things a man chooses or avoids."
~ Aristotle[28]

So far we have learned that ethics by themselves are not enough to achieve integrity. Likewise, virtues alone are just good works. Character is the link between beliefs and actions, making it possible to become an excellent person. Character is about why you do what you do, more than how you think and what you do. It is the next step toward integrity: who you are.

In his book *Chivalry-Now*, D. Joseph Jacques wrote: "The subject of character runs deeper than how we act or what we believe. It strikes the very core of our being. ... The building of one's character is nothing less than claiming possession of one's soul. ... Build thyself. If we do not, others will do the work for us, according to their own haphazard design."[10]

97

Plato and character

We match the three classic Greek philosophers as proponents of the Three Steps to Integrity; Aristotle for virtues, Socrates for ethics, and Plato for character. Plato (c. 428–348 B.C.) founded the Academy in Athens, the first institution of higher learning in the Western world. Along with Socrates, his teacher, and Aristotle, his student, Plato established the fundamentals of Western philosophy. Many of Plato's dialogues examine the nature of virtue and the character of a virtuous person. The Greek philosophers utilized character to explain virtues. It takes someone of strong moral character to determine with consistency and dependability what actions (virtues) are appropriate and reasonable.

"The ABC Model" adapts Plato's use of character in what we identify as the moral fiber that connects ethics (beliefs) and virtues (actions).

Plato placed an emphasis on being rather than just doing. Morality stems from your character identity, rather than being a reflection of the actions alone. This is critically needed for integrity, because it demonstrates that just as ethics translate into virtues, without character, beliefs and actions alone fail. Integrity requires ethics, virtues and character, all three.

What character is and is not

The Merriam-Webster Dictionary[26] defines character as:

- One of the attributes or features that make up and distinguish an individual.
- The aggregate features and traits that form the individual nature of some person or thing.
- Moral excellence and firmness.
- Your reputation.

The word character comes from the Greek word referring to an image on a coin. That is appropriate, as your image is how consistently you live out your ethics and virtues. Everyone has character. Some think of character as something a person either has or does not have. "He has character," typically means a person has moral character. We assert that everyone has character, but distinguish between good and bad character.

Character demonstrates consistency between what you say you will do and what you actually do. Character includes actions you take to carry out the values, ethics and morals you believe in. If ethics are your system of beliefs and goals, and virtues are your actions and behavior, then character is that which stands between beliefs and actions; the "moral fiber" governing "why" you do what you do.

Examples of character

What are the character qualities, or character traits that make up a person's character? How can they be built into a person's life? Can they be changed? If you make a list of good "character qualities," or "character traits," you probably will include such words as honesty, integrity, dependability, loyalty, enthusiasm, etc. Of course, there are many others that could be added.

The Character Training Institute (CTI) of Oklahoma City, Oklahoma constructed a list of character traits. CTI breaks character down into forty-nine specific character qualities or traits. Notice this list contains what we have already identified as ethics and virtues. However, having such a list of character traits allows you to focus on the specific qualities in building your "good character".

1. **Alertness** (Being aware of what is taking place around me so I can have the right responses)
2. **Attentiveness** (Showing the worth of a person or task by giving my undivided concentration)
3. **Availability** (Making my schedule and priorities secondary to the wishes of those I serve)
4. **Benevolence** (Giving to others' basic needs without having as my motive personal reward)
5. **Boldness** (Confidence to say or do what is true, right, and just)
6. **Cautiousness** (Knowing the importance of right timing in accomplishing right actions)
7. **Compassion** (Investing whatever is necessary to heal the hurts of others)
8. **Contentment** (Realizing that true happiness does not depend on material conditions)
9. **Creativity** (Approaching a need, a task, or an idea from a new perspective)

10. **Decisiveness** (The ability to recognize key factors and finalize difficult decisions)
11. **Deference** (Limiting my freedom so I do not offend the tastes of those around me)
12. **Dependability** (Fulfilling what I consented to do, even if it means unexpected sacrifice)
13. **Determination** (Purposing to accomplish right goals at the right time, regardless of the opposition)
14. **Diligence** (Investing all my energy to complete the tasks assigned to me)
15. **Discernment** (Understanding the deeper reasons why things happen)
16. **Discretion** (Recognizing and avoiding words, actions, and attitudes that could bring undesirable consequences)
17. **Endurance** (The inward strength to withstand stress and do my best)
18. **Enthusiasm** (Expressing joy in each task as I give it my best effort)
19. **Faith** (Confidence that actions rooted in good character will yield the best outcome, even when I cannot see how)
20. **Flexibility** (Willingness to change plans or ideas without getting upset)
21. **Forgiveness** (Clearing the record of those who have wronged me and not holding a grudge)
22. **Generosity** (Carefully managing my resources so I can freely give to those in need)
23. **Gentleness** (Showing consideration and personal concern for others)
24. **Gratefulness** (Letting others know by my words and actions how they have benefited my life)
25. **Honor** (Respecting others because of their worth as human beings)
26. **Hospitality** (Cheerfully sharing food, shelter, and friendship with others)
27. **Humility** (Acknowledging that achievement results from the investment of others in my life)
28. **Initiative** (Recognizing and doing what needs to be done before I am asked to do it)
29. **Joyfulness** (Maintaining a good attitude, even when faced with unpleasant) conditions)

30. **Justice** (Taking personal responsibility to uphold what is pure, right, and true)
31. **Loyalty** (Using difficult times to demonstrate my commitment to those I serve)
32. **Meekness** (Yielding my personal rights and expectations with a desire to serve)
33. **Obedience** (Quickly and cheerfully carrying out the direction of those who are responsible for me)
34. **Orderliness** (Arranging myself and my surroundings to achieve greater efficiency)
35. **Patience** (Accepting a difficult situation without giving a deadline to remove it)
36. **Persuasiveness** (Guiding vital truths around another's mental roadblocks)
37. **Punctuality** (Showing esteem for others by doing the right thing at the right time)
38. **Resourcefulness** (Making wise use of what others might overlook or discard)
39. **Responsibility** (Knowing and doing what is expected of me)
40. **Security** (Structuring my life around that which cannot be destroyed or taken away)
41. **Self-Control** (Rejecting wrong desires and doing what is right)
42. **Sensitivity** (Using my senses to perceive the true attitudes and emotions of others
43. **Sincerity** (Eagerly doing what is right with transparent motives)
44. **Thoroughness** (Knowing what factors will diminish the effectiveness of my work or words, if neglected)
45. **Thriftiness** (Allowing myself and others to spend only what is necessary)
46. **Tolerance** (Accepting others at different levels of maturity)
47. **Truthfulness** (Earning future trust by accurately reporting past facts)
48. **Virtue** (The moral excellence evident in my life as I consistently do what is right)
49. **Wisdom** (Making practical applications of truth in daily decisions)

By breaking character down into its basic elements and traits in this way, you are better able to focus on building specific qualities into your life. As you work on strengthening particular good character qualities, your overall character improves. For example, "honesty" consists of several more basic qualities – truthfulness, dependability, reliability, etc. Therefore, when I work on becoming more honest, I do so by becoming more truthful, more dependable, and more reliable, etc.

Why your character is important

Take a look at the character of today's society: escalating crime, workplace violence, gang activity, drug and alcohol abuse, vandalism, school dropouts, deteriorating work ethics, domestic violence, juvenile delinquency, racial tensions, broken families. The list is extensive. All of these problems emerge from a root cause: the lack of good character. Without character development, the future looks rather bleak.

Your benefits and risks of character

Many business leaders are learning that character training is essential for lasting success in business. Focusing only on profit without emphasizing character is a losing proposition. Employees who are more honest, responsible, and trustworthy will undoubtedly become much more successful, and so will the enterprise.

Character development is essential to the ongoing success of your society. That is why character education is so crucial. Character is the foundation and key to success! You may have money, position, or power, but unless you have good character, you will not be truly successful.

On a more immediate and practical level, your character is what determines your success in any area of life. Your character is what guides your responses to any situation or circumstance in your life. How you respond to the various things that come up daily is what determines the results you get.

How to build your personal character

Every person may become a person of strong character. It is a matter of choice. Each of us is responsible for our thoughts and conduct. Developing new ethical and positive habits is your responsibility. Thomas Paine said, "Character is much easier kept than recovered."[25] That means once you develop strong character you must work to maintain it. Just as different virtues reinforce each other, different character traits reinforce each other, helping to create an inner life of fidelity.

Benjamin Franklin developed a strategy for building character that included thirteen character qualities that he felt necessary to improve his life. He focused attention on each character trait for one week at a time. That meant he gave attention to improving each character trait four weeks out of every year. Some of his character traits were what we identify as virtues. Others are excellent habits. Franklin's character traits included:

- Self-control - be determined and disciplined in your efforts.
- Silence - listen better in all discussions.
- Order – don't agonize - organize.
- Pledge - promise to put your best effort into today's activities.
- Thrift - watch how you spend your money and your time.
- Productive - work hard - work smart - have fun.
- Fairness - treat others the way you want to be treated.
- Moderation - avoid extremes.
- Cleanliness - have clean mind, body, and habits.
- Tranquility - take time to slow down and smell the roses.
- Charity - help others.
- Humility - keep your ego in check.
- Sincerity - be honest with yourself and others.

You should strive to understand as much as possible about the character quality and how it can be applied to your own life situations. You should also seek to live your life as if you fully possessed the character standard upon which you are focusing. You should be aware of how the character quality (or the lack of it) is demonstrated in the lives of those around you and evaluate the results and consequences you see in their lives.

The Six Pillars of Character[11] in "CHARACTER COUNTS" by Josephson Institute of Ethics teach children the importance of character, including:

Citizenship

- Do your share to make your school and community better
- Cooperate
- Get involved in community affairs
- Stay informed; vote
- Be a good neighbor
- Obey laws and rules
- Respect authority
- Protect the environment
- Volunteer

Chapter 8

Character and Your Habits

"Our character is basically a composite of our habits.
Because they are consistent, often unconscious
patterns, they constantly, daily, express our character."
~ Stephen Covey[4]

Have you heard the old saying, "We are creatures of habit."?
Think for a moment of someone who has poor habits.
Maybe it is a co-worker who does his/her work carelessly. Maybe
it is a relative who continually makes "poor choices".

My wife gave me a clipping with a familiar quotation:

"Watch your thoughts, for they become words.
Watch your words, for they become actions.
Watch your actions, for they become habits.
Watch your habits, for they become character.
Watch your character, for it becomes your destiny." (Anon)

Aristotle said much the same thing as he wrestled with under-standing ethics and integrity. "We are what we repeatedly do. Excellence, then, is not an act, but a habit."[28]

Habits are not blind routines, reducing life to a series of rather boring, but good, routines. The word Aristotle used for habit is virtue. That is why developing good habits is, as he put it, the only way to experience the good life, or what he identified as "happiness". We all have good habits and bad habits. We struggle to get rid of the bad ones, and work to develop more of the good ones.

Here are some ideas that may be useful as you consider your habits.

- Do not be guided by your feelings and emotions. (Your feelings may be the worst enemy of good habits)
- Do what is right. (Have the courage to do the right thing, even if it is unpopular or difficult)
- Do what needs doing now, not tomorrow. (Don't procrastinate)
- Do what you do to the best of your ability. (Don't settle for less than excellence, even in small tasks)
- Do what you do for the right reason. (Don't act out of jealousy, anger, malice, etc.)
- Do not cut corners. (Most tragedies– the Shuttle explosion, the BP disaster - occur when someone takes a short cut and does not "completely" do their job)
- Do choose wisely. (Habits are choices, and no one else is responsible for your habits)
- Do discipline yourself. (While we should not delay in doing tasks, we should learn to delay gratification – as in saving for retirement, not eating a dessert that has more calories than the meal, etc.)
- Do enjoy what you do. (Although it requires effort to do your best, you will reap the rewards that only come from giving it your best effort)
- Do what you do "heartily" and "mightily":
  o "Whatever you do, work at it with all your heart, as working for the Lord, not for men." (Colossians 3:23 NIV)
  o "Whatever your hand finds to do, do it with all your might, for in the grave, where you are going, there is neither working nor planning nor knowledge nor wisdom." (Ecclesiastes 9:10 NIV)

When you develop the habit of doing the right thing, in the right way, at the right time, for the right reason, it becomes easier for you to develop more good habits, and improve the ones you already have. Good habits become your routine, or norm; and they become your character. Ethics are how you think (beliefs, values, principles and ideals). Your virtues are your actions, your habits. Your habits reveal who you are; your character and integrity.

For Aristotle, ethics were not theoretical exercises. Virtues of character are the habits of behaving in a certain way. Thus, good conduct arises from habits that in turn can only be acquired by repeated action and correction, making ethics an intensely practical discipline. "We do not act rightly because we have virtue or excellence, but we rather have those because we have acted rightly," he said.[28]

Habit and Trait

Virtues align closely with habits or traits. The two are not entirely interchangeable. We should distinguish between habits and traits. For instance, a habit of having a morning cup of coffee does not equate to a character trait. Likewise, honesty is not just a tendency (habit) to do what is honest. It is a deeply entrenched character trait. The disposition of honesty involves many other actions, with emotions, temperament, etc. You cannot ascribe a virtue on the basis of a single action.

Not all habits are character traits, but character traits are well-entrenched habits that contribute to virtues. That is not to say, as Aristotle would argue, that virtues are not habits. As stated earlier, virtues are the habit of doing things that lead to the Good.

A character quality is a habit, a standard method or way of thinking, speaking or behavior. Like other habits, good character traits can be developed, and undesirable character traits eliminated, by repeatedly making decisions and taking actions that reinforce the pattern of good character traits. Anne Frank said, "The final forming of a person's character lies in their own hands."[28]

Stephen Covey wrote, "Our character is basically a composite of our habits. Because they are consistent, often unconscious patterns, they constantly, daily, express our character."[4]

Chapter 9

Character and Your Motives

"It is futile to judge a kind deed by its motives.
Kindness can become its own motive.
We are made kind by being kind."
~ Eric Hoffer[28]

Would you be surprised that researchers have found the reason you do something is as important as doing it? Apparently, our motives are as important as our actions. A 2011 study conducted at the University of Michigan shows that WHY people volunteer (not whether they volunteer) is what really counts. The study, published by the American Psychological Association's Health Psychology, found those who volunteer and give out of pure motives, such as compassion or simply to help others, live longer than those who do not volunteer at all, or who do so for personal benefit, such as getting their picture in the newspaper or personal acclaim. Even after controlling for variables that influence mortality, such as physical health, the researchers found that motives for volunteering still have an impact on how long and how well we live.27 That is not to say volunteers should never expect any benefit for their efforts. But now there is research to show "pure motives" provide the greatest benefit of all: a longer and happier (less stressful) life.

Motives are an essential component of character. While "how we think" and "what we do" are extremely important, the motives for connecting our beliefs and actions get to the heart of "who we are". It is a key indicator of our moral fiber.

"All a man's ways seem innocent to him,
but motives are weighed by the LORD."
~ Proverbs 16:2

Mankind sees and judges from outward appearances. That is why we are often surprised, disappointed or even betrayed when the motives of one's heart becomes public. Abraham Maslow put it this way: "But behavior in the human being is sometimes a defense, a way of concealing motives and thoughts, as language can be a way of hiding your thoughts and preventing communication."

In the Sermon on the Mount, Jesus said 2000 years ago: "So when you give to the needy, do not announce it with trumpets, as the hypocrites do in the synagogues and on the streets, to be honored by others. Truly I tell you, they have received their reward in full. But when you give to the needy, do not let your left hand know what your right hand is doing, so that your giving may be in secret. Then your Father, who sees what is done in secret, will reward you." (Matthew 6:2-4 NIV).

So, what is your motive? If it is to gain something, then you may obtain your reward. But if it is to do the right thing, because it is right, and to do it for the right reason, at the right time and in the right way with excellence, then the doing becomes its own reward. Your motives disclose your character and surprisingly improve your life's quality and span.

Motivation is literally the desire to get things done; to set and accomplish goals. Research shows you can influence your own motivation to decide what you want to achieve and become who you want to be.

Among the enemies of motivation are:

- Lack of consistency - Fits of idleness and overachieving.
- Lack of confidence – Convincing yourself, "I'll never be able to do that".
- Lack of focus – Uncertainty of what you want, especially right now!

- Lack of direction – Uncertainty of how to achieve your goals.

If you want to excel and succeed in life, self-motivation is essential. You must know the keys to motivate yourself. You must be able to persist in the midst of difficulty. Andrew Carnegie said, "People who are unable to motivate themselves must be content with mediocrity, no matter how impressive their other talents."[28]

Chapter 10

Character as Responsibility

"You cannot escape the responsibility
of tomorrow by evading it today."
~ Abraham Lincoln[28]

As a member of an organization's board, I became frustrated that at each monthly meeting, we seemed to discuss the same problems over and over. One problem in particular took up considerable time at every meeting, but no one took responsibility for solving the problem. The board unknowingly was playing a game called "Oh, ain't it awful?" It is a lot of fun, but totally meaningless, and potentially deadly for a business. You get to complain, blame, and whine that someone else is not doing their job.

Finally, I had enough. Although it was not in my chain of command, or certainly not my expertise, I said, "I'll understand this problem and see what I can do to fix it." No one objected. I threw myself into the mix, took a steep learning curve, found the problem, and more importantly, found a solution. Now that board can deal with more weighty issues.

Taking responsibility is liberating. It is the only way to resolve mistakes, solve problems, learn from experience, and move on to a more productive life.

You must take responsibility for every aspect of your life. Do not blame circumstances or individuals for anything in your life for which you are not satisfied. Owning your life and the way you live it is not only a hallmark of integrity, but the keystone of maturity. Only you can change the things you do not want in your life.

Keys to Taking Responsibility

The Serenity Prayer
God grant me the serenity
to accept the things I cannot change
courage to change the things I can
and wisdom to know the difference. (Anon)

Take responsibility

"The price of greatness is responsibility."
~ Winston Churchill[28]

1. Take responsibility for your decisions.
Accept that you are solely responsible for your choices and decisions in life. Life is a series of decisions, big and small. Every time you make a decision, make it based on the best information you have at that time, and factor in such things as 'is this right and lawful?' 'Will it hurt someone?' Make the best decision that you can, given the information you have and the situation at the time. Then move forward and spend your time trying to make that decision work. Do not waste time regretting past decisions (as in, I should/shouldn't have married xxx, or I never should have left xxx; or I am so sorry I ever took this job, etc.). Regret is a tremendous time-waster and only serves to hold you back and make you doubt yourself. Yes, some decisions will turn out to be mistakes in the long run, but they probably were the best choice at the time, or you would not have chosen that option. No one thinks about a decision and then says "I am going to choose option B, even though it is not as good as option A". Do not make decisions without thinking about them. Make the best decision that you can, given the situation at the time. If it turns out to be a mistake, learn from that mistake. Take ownership of your decisions and do not abdicate them to others. Certainly it is smart to seek advice

from those with wisdom, but do not let other people make decisions for you. Own your decisions because you are the one who has to live with their consequences.

"You may believe that you are responsible for what you do, but not for what you think. The truth is that you are responsible for what you think, because it is only at this level that you can exercise choice. What you do comes from what you think."

— Marianne Williamson, Return to Love (Leadershipnow.com)

2. Take responsibility for your actions and inaction.

This includes everything we have done, and the things we left undone that we should have done. If you are "waiting for the cavalry to arrive", or hoping someone on a white horse will suddenly swoop in and save the situation, you must stop procrastinating. Taking responsibility means acknowledging both your weaknesses and strengths.

3. Take responsibility for your happiness and your future.

Taking responsibility for yourself is one of the most liberating things you can do. You no longer see yourself the victim of circumstances. Realize you can accomplish anything you set your mind to do. It is a liberating concept. Help may not be coming. The responsibility is yours, and it starts with developing a belief or habit of mind that you, as an individual, are accountable for the quality and timeliness of an outcome, even when you are working with others. It does not always mean you have authority over a project. Nor does it mean that you should not involve others. But it does mean you own the obligation to take action and deliver results.

Be accountable

1. Recognize that accountability and responsibility are not the same.

Accountability is a major part of responsibility. Understand how they relate, and how they differ.

Responsibility can be given, received or assumed, but that does not guarantee that you accept personal accountability. It is possible to accept responsibility for something but still lack accountability. You can be given responsibility, but you have to take accountability. One is bestowed and assumed; the other must be personally acquired. Accountability is something you do to yourself, not something that someone does to you.

RACI is a methodology especially useful in defining roles and responsibilities. The acronym represents the four key responsibilities in project management or business process: Responsible, Accountable, Consulted, and Informed. RACI delineates the difference between responsibility and accountability.

- **The Responsible person** - Those who do the work to accomplish the task. There is typically one responsible person, although others can be delegated to assist in the work required.
- **The Accountable person** (also approver or final approving authority) - The one ultimately answerable for the correct and thorough completion of the deliverable or task, and the one who delegates the work to those responsible. In other words, an accountable person must sign off (approve) on work that the responsible person provides. There must be only one accountable person specified for each task or deliverable.
- **Consulted** (sometimes counsel) - Those whose opinions are sought, typically subject matter experts; and with whom there is two-way communication.
- **Informed** - Those who are kept up-to-date on progress, often only on completion of the task or deliverable; and with whom there is just one-way communication.[31]

Learn from your mistakes, and use that knowledge to avoid doing the same thing again. Someone who says "I take responsibility for that" and then continues to do the same sort of thing over and over has not taken responsibility.

2. Where possible, "make amends" for past mistakes.

Acknowledge what happened. If you broke something, fix it, as much as possible. Apologize. Speak the truth.

3. Admit and accept responsibility for your mistakes

"If you mess up, 'fess up." Sophocles long ago said, "It is a painful thing to look at your own trouble and know that you yourself and no one else has made it."[28] Accepting responsibilities include accepting fault, if you are at fault. But do not dwell on fault. Fault is backward-looking, and responsibility is forward-looking. Fixating on blame does no good. Focusing on responsibility is liberating. But just saying "I take responsibility for that" is not taking responsibility. There are a number of people who might claim responsibility for something, but that is all they do. Saying you are responsible is only the first step in taking responsibility for something negative. The next part is investigating what you can do to "fix" the problem, and then doing it. Frequently, it may require apologizing to someone as well.

Do not Play "The Blame Game"

1. Your parents/family/the past: It is a plus if you had wonderful parents and siblings—the majority of people do not. Many unpleasant or unhappy things may have happened during your childhood. The past is the past, and until time travel is perfected, there is no way of changing it. You just have to deal with whatever happened then and learn from the bad. I never understand why a child who is abused, grows up to abuse their own children. Or, a child who grows up in an alcoholic/drug family goes on to become a substance abuser. If you have had bad experiences in your life, use those to define what you do not want in your future life. Do not go on to become the bad parents, use those negative experiences to become the opposite of the bad

for your own children—or do not choose to have children if you cannot. Quit using past circumstances as excuses for poor decisions and actions in the present.

2. **Your significant other:** It is a losing proposition to blame your significant other for negative aspects of your life. Remember that at some point you chose that person(s). If you blame your significant other, it only increases the negativity in the relationship and then the relationship is destined to failure at some point anyhow. If your significant other actually is bringing a negative aspect into your life, then quit blaming them and choose to leave. It is up to only you if you stay in a bad relationship. Own your relationship choices.

3. **Your children:** Some people see their children as some kind of obstacle or negative in their life. They think, if only I did not have the children, 'I would have more money to live the kind of life I want', or 'I could have gone to college' or "I would be able to attract the companion of my choice'. And some people have children with physical or emotional problems, which is a strain on anyone. Remember at some point, you participated in the decision to have children, and they are your responsibility for at least 18 years. Blaming them does not help them or you. Focus on the positives of being a parent and the positives about each child, and do your best to encourage them to become responsible adults and members of society. The right attitude toward your parenthood can bring you many positives, and be the greatest aspect of your life. Or, you can choose to be unhappy or dissatisfied about it, and make everyone's life worse. Own your parenting choices.

4. **Your boss/co-workers:** I never had a bad job—but there were many where I did not like some of the people I had to work with. Again, remember that at some point you chose to take the job. If you cannot turn the situation around at work, then start looking for another job. If you have bad relationships at every job you take, then start looking at yourself for why the working relationships are poor. Own your job choices.

5. **The President/Republicans/Democrats/Tea Party:** It is easy to whine about the economy, taxes, foreign policy,

etc. It may actually be that the economy and other factors outside your control are bringing negative aspects to your life. This is one of those places, where you have to say to yourself, "Is there anything I can do about it?" Mostly, the answer is no. But what you can do is quit complaining, campaign and vote for candidates who you think will be an improvement; and above all, be the best citizen you can be as an example to others.

6. **God/fate:** Some people blame God (or "fate" for nonbelievers) for negative aspects of their lives. Perhaps it gives them a good feeling to blame someone or something other than themselves for their problems. It is another way of wallowing in your misery instead of doing something about it. If you were honest with yourself, in 99% of the cases, you can see how a series of decisions on your part led you to the bad place. Recognize it, own it, and change it.

7. **Yourself:** You might find this strange to be on this list after saying 'own your life', and 'take responsibility for your choices'. The overall point of this is that blame is counter-productive to everything positive. Do not blame circumstances, other people, or yourself. Everyone makes mistakes. It is a normal part of life and a necessity to learning. Learn from your mistakes. There is nothing shameful about mistakes if you try to fix them (if possible) and you learn from them. What is shameful is making the same mistakes over and over again.

Do not waste time "blaming"; it serves no useful purpose.

Responsibility

- Do what you are supposed to do.
- Plan ahead.
- Persevere: keep on trying!
- Always do your best.
- Use self-control.
- Be self-disciplined.
- Think before you act — consider the consequences.
- Be accountable for your words, actions, and attitudes.
- Set a good example for others.

Conclusion

What will taking responsibility do for my life and character? Living with responsibility will allow you to

- Move beyond past mistakes.
- It will give you a new start.
- Be stronger.
- Be more productive.
- Be more respected.

You cannot change the circumstances, but you can change yourself. You are the only one in charge of you! It is up to you to make changes and take responsibility for outcomes in your life. What are you waiting for?

Chapter 11

Character as Excellence

"If you focus on success, you'll have stress.
But if you pursue excellence, success will be guaranteed."
~ Deepak Chopra[2]

Mrs. Shaw, a fourth grade teacher, wrote on his final report card: "William is not living up to his potential. He can do much better work." What hurt most was William knew she was correct. He was doing average work, good enough to get him promoted from the fourth to fifth grade. But he was not doing his best. His coursework was not excellent.

What is excellence? Is it having more wins than losses? Or, is it more than one accomplishment; a never-ending process of striving to do your very best? Aristotle once said, "Excellence is an art won by training and habituation. We do not act rightly because we have virtue or excellence, but we rather have those because we have acted rightly. We are what we repeatedly do. Excellence, then, is not an act but a habit."[25]

Ten Principles for Personal Excellence

1. Have a passion for excellence

Have a dream! Review the ideals of your personal ethics (Chapter 4). Strive to achieve those ideals, not just by the skin of your teeth; but because you want to achieve your ideals with excellence. Have the passion to become excellent, or else you resign yourself to a second-best life. To borrow the slogan of the U.S. Army, "Be all you can be."

2. Have a plan for excellence

Setting a goal without proper planning is like setting off for a destination without a roadmap and resources to get there. Every goal needs a strategy and plan for success. Most goals fail in the planning stage. Becoming excellent is one of the most important goals of life. It requires that you invest proper time and effort in building your plan. Make sure your goals include:

- Aiming for your very best in whatever you set out to do
- Never accepting second best work from yourself or your team
- Reaching your highest human potential

3. Measure by your potential, not others' potential

There is an adage, "Good is the enemy of the best." You may do a job better than anyone else in your area, but if you could have done an even better job, you have not measured up to excellence. You may have talents that make it easy to just get by. Deep inside, you know when you have done your very best; when your efforts have been excellent. You also know when you cut corners, procrastinated, took the easy road or turned in a less than excellent performance. You know when you work to just pass the test and get a C-, and you know when you give it all you have, and get an A+.

4. Benchmark against the best

While you measure by your own potential, you also benchmark against the best. Perform against known external standards, mentors, and the "best of breed". The emphasis here is on what you want, not what others want. For example, if your football team has a 5-5 win-loss record, it is easy to compare them against the 4-6 teams. But how do they measure up against the 10-0 team? How do they compare to the National Champion? Always strive to be the best, not just good.

5. Do not confuse busyness with excellence.

The person of excellence is a person of the highest effectiveness and efficiency. In its earliest appearance in Greek, this notion of excellence connected with the notion of the fulfillment of purpose or function: the act of living up to one's full potential. For instance, a cup is excellent to the degree it fulfills the purpose of being a cup. If the cup does not "hold water" or inhibits taking a drink, then it is not excellent. Becoming an over-achiever or workaholic means you cannot devote the time and energy in the one or two areas where you most likely can achieve excellence. Remember:

- Effectiveness is doing the right thing
- Efficiency is doing the right thing well

6. Focus on your gifts and make them excellent

You are unique, an individual, one of a kind. No one is exactly like you, not even if you are a twin. So achieving excellence in your life is a very personal endeavor. You should focus on who you ought to be and what you want to accomplish in life. For instance, trying to become a concert pianist is terrific if you have musical skills and a gift for playing the piano. For someone who is tone deaf, nonmusical, and has poor manual dexterity, such an effort would be futile and a waste of time and talent. You are in this world to do something no one else can do as well as you. Focusing on your gifts, which normally means doing what you really enjoy doing, is the only way to find fulfillment of purpose and function; exactly what the Greek philosophers called excellence.

7. Be committed to excellence in yourself and your team.

Success comes from hard work. Those who seek the easy way out are fooling themselves if they think they can achieve excellence without hard work. Those who follow the easy road or "get rich quick" strategies are the ones who achieve little of value in life. Hard work is the universal quality required for success and excellence. It always pays off in the end.

8. Never stop improving and learning.

Connect with the best people in your field of endeavor and learn from them. They have already learned the best practices, skills, insights and guidelines which you will find valuable in your pursuit of excellence. The apprentice learns skills from the master that will save him or her years of trial and error. The Greeks explicitly linked the highest human potential (excellence) with knowledge. We call such knowledge wisdom or understanding. We all hope our doctors are keeping up with the latest medical knowledge, no matter if they are nearing retirement. Why should you do less? To stop learning in life is to stop striving for excellence.

9. Be consistent

Do not give your best one day, and take the easy road the next. Becoming an excellent person means consistency, with the virtue of trustworthiness – someone who can be relied upon. Do not give your life half-hearted efforts. You and your life are too valuable for that. And do the hard work FIRST!

10. Believe you can become excellent NOW!

You must believe that you can achieve excellence. Remember that everyone has human potential. Excellence is possible, if you want it, are willing to do the hard work, and ready to receive the rewards. Successful living and leading start now: Accept the challenge to "Be All You Can Be".

John Maxwell provided some powerful tools for achieving your best in his book, *Be All You Can Be*[16]. You may see some of the Ten Principles for Personal Excellence stated in a different way in Maxwell's four key steps to help you discover the principles of success that can actually help you succeed.

- **Know:** Discover the principles for fulfilling your God-given potential.
- **Show:** Learn how to model the principles so others can see them at work.
- **Go:** Roll up your sleeves, get out into the world, and live what you have learned.
- **Grow:** Experience living at your full potential, continually assessing your progress.

And by the way, my fourth grade teacher was Mrs. Shaw. And my first name is William.

"Finally, brethren, whatever is true, whatever is
honorable, whatever is just, whatever is pure, whatever
is lovely, whatever is gracious, if there is any excellence,
if there is anything worthy of praise, think about these
things."
~ Paul's Epistle to the Philippians

Chapter 12

Character as Honor

"Who sows virtue reaps honor."
~ Leonardo da Vinci

Plato long ago noted, "There are three classes of men; lovers of wisdom, lovers of honor, and lovers of gain."[28] Honor will not suddenly appear in your life by accident. You must make honor a primary goal.

So, what is honor? Is it the same as your reputation or respect? Is it a character trait, like honesty? Do we live in a post-honor culture? Honor is a subjective evaluation of your composite character traits by others, especially your peers and those closest to you. In that sense, honor is not so much something you do, as with virtues, but something you acquire through consistent adherence to a set standard of ethics and conduct, or an honor code. An honor code is a set of principles or rules, seen mostly in military and academic settings, defining what constitutes honorable behavior.

Honor is not the same as morality. It is quite possible to live a moral life without achieving honor. That is true in part because we measure morality more in what you do not do (lie, cheat, steal) than what you do (character traits, virtues). Remember the adage "There is no honor among thieves". That means you cannot have honor in one area of your life while living in dishonor in another area.

Reputation and your "good name"

We distinguish between reputation and character. Thomas Paine put it this way, "Reputation is what men and women think of us. Character is what God and the angels know of us."[28] Your reputation is the opinion or identity defined by others. Abraham Lincoln said, "Character is like a tree and reputation like a shadow. The shadow is what we think of it; the tree is the real thing."[28]

"A good name is rather to be chosen than great riches." (Proverbs 22:1) The Book of Proverbs emphasizes that your reputation is worth more than a fortune. Put another way, you cannot buy a good reputation. You may lose your health or wealth, and with considerable effort may regain them. In this hyper-connected world, a rumor can "go viral" in minutes. But if you lose your reputation, it will be most difficult to get it back. Your "good name" is one of the most valuable attributes you have. A person of honor knows the value of a hard-earned reputation and will guard it diligently. Most people, however, spend more time planning their vacation than improving and protecting their reputation.

Your character is more than what others see of you; character gets to why you do what you do, and begins to reveal who you are inside, especially when no one is watching. Good character is doing the right thing because it is the right thing to do. (For more on reputation, see the chapter on Honor.)

Respect

Respect is one of the hallmarks of honor and very important. We remember Aretha Franklin best for her hit song, "R-E-S-P-E-C-T". Respect is bigger in some cultures than others. There are places even in the United States where you can get yourself killed for "disrespecting" someone. Rodney Dangerfield built his comedy career around the phrase, "I get no respect". Respect is regard or esteem for the character qualities (good judgment, courage, honesty, etc.) for the one respected, or for conduct in harmony with a specific ethic or virtue. The opposite of respect is contempt or mere tolerance. You earn respect by doing the right thing, by being honest, fair and trustworthy.

In the Six Pillars of Character[11] in "Character Counts" by the Josephson Institute of Ethics teach children the elements of respect:

- Treat others with respect; follow the Golden Rule.
- Be tolerant and accepting of differences.
- Use good manners, not bad language.
- Be considerate of the feelings of others.
- Do not threaten, hit or hurt anyone.
- Deal peacefully with anger, insults, and disagreements.

Duty: Going Above and Beyond

Honor is not just meeting expectations, but going "above and beyond the call of duty". Duty carries a sense of moral commitment or obligation to someone or something. That moral commitment is not a passive feeling; it must result in action. When you recognize a duty, you commit yourself to its fulfillment without considering your self-interests. Duty almost always involves some type of self-sacrifice.

Cicero, in his work "On Duty", suggested that duties come as a result of:

- Your being human (certain duty accrue to being human)
- Your particular place in life (duties related to family, nation, occupation, profession)
- Your character (duties that must be done because they are right)
- Your moral expectations for yourself (duties from your character and integrity)

Dignity

Aristotle said, "The ideal man bears the accidents of life with dignity and grace, making the best of circumstances."[28] This means the honorable person does not blame others, get angry, carry grudges, speak out of hate, act unkindly or vindictively, etc. When you deal with a difficult situation with maturity, professionalism, and out of a sense of caring, others will see you as a person of honor.

Honor establishes your personal dignity and character. Dignity signifies that a person has an inborn right to respect and ethical treatment. It is an extension of the concepts of "inalienable rights". Dignity and respect are closely linked. A judge will speak about the dignity of the court, which means the lawyers, plaintiffs, defendants, and spectators must show the proper decorum such dignity demands. Dignity is a quality of conduct. Each election year, we compare candidates for "Who looks most presidential?" That means, who conducts him/herself most in accord with the dignity of the office. Dignity is often used in conjunction with grace, as Aristotle did. You probably hear such remarks as, "He handled that difficult situation with dignity and grace." Both dignity and grace, in this context, have to do with those qualities of character shown in handling the challenges of life with integrity.

"Noblesse oblige"

Noblesse oblige (nobility obligation) advocates that a noble person is obliged to honorable behavior, and such privilege requires the more fortunate to help the less fortunate with courtesy and respect. It tracks the Biblical admonition, "For unto whom much is given, of him shall be much required". (Luke 12:48). "Noblesse oblige" nowadays refers more often to situations wherein a person's position requires obligations from them, such as a supervisor feels a degree of "noblesse oblige" to attend one of their subordinate's birthday lunch or retirement party.

Ethically, privilege must be balanced by duty towards those who lack such privilege or who cannot perform such duty. The rich, famous and powerful incur responsibilities to provide good examples of behavior and standards of decency. A person of honor will exemplify honorable behavior and help the less fortunate with both courtesy and respect. That is why you see many celebrities take on moral causes or charitable interests. You do not have to possess privilege or fame to be honorable. Any person in any situation can demonstrate nobility through their behavior and actions.

Chivalry

Perhaps the best examples of honor were displayed in Medieval Chivalry. King Arthur and the Knights of the Round Table held noble honor as the apex of character. After years of studying Arthurian literature from a cultural perspective, D. Joseph Jacques wrote the following principles in his book, *Chivalry-Now: The Code of Male Ethics*, establishing a new Code of Chivalry appropriate for our times, which he calls:

"The Twelve Trusts"[10]

"Upon my honor...

1. I will develop my life for the greater good.
2. I will place character about riches and concern for others about personal wealth.
3. I will never boast but cherish humility instead.
4. I will speak the truth at all times and forever keep my word.
5. I will defend those who cannot defend themselves.
6. I will honor and respect women and refute sexism in all its guises.
7. I will uphold justice by being fair to all.
8. I will be faithful in love and loyal in friendship.
9. I will abhor scandal and gossip - neither partake nor delight in them.
10. I will be generous to the poor and to those who need help.
11. I will forgive when asked that my own mistakes will be forgiven.
12. I will live my life of courtesy and honor from this day forward."

Jacques[10] continued and listed some examples of what honor is not:

- There is no honor in boasting and belittling other people.
- There is no honor in dulling one's mind and judgment with alcohol or drugs. Doing so detracts from completeness and clarity of mind.
- There is no honor in harming innocent people, in victimizing or controlling women, or placing profit ahead of compassion.
- There is no honor in telling people lies or delighting in gossip or slander.
- There is no honor in smearing an opponent, political or otherwise, with false allegations.
- There is no honor in cheating or breaking promises.
- There is no honor in complacency in the face of injustice, especially when opportunity calls for bold action.

- There is no honor in winning when it compromises the integrity of your soul.
- There is no honor in being false concerning matters of love.

Honor and honors

Honor as a quality of your character should be thought of differently from the honors you may earn. For instance, an athlete may win a gold medal for her excellent performance at the Olympics. That honor is not the same as her honor. Honors, in this sense, are external validations of skills or accomplishments. Honor is an internal state achieved by adherence to a code of honor.

That is not to say that honors are not a factor in honor. A well-decorated soldier may be justly proud of the emblems on his uniform. But he most likely will be the first to say his honor is greater than the honors he has earned. Likewise, a Doctor of Philosophy may be justly proud of the degree hanging on her wall. That degree is but one factor in honor of her character. Socrates rebuked the citizens of Athens who were absorbed in accumulating wealth, reputation, and honors while they did not care nor strive for wisdom, truth, and the betterment of their souls. Rather than heaping up riches and honors, he encouraged the Athenians to perfect their souls in virtue. By doing so, honor will follow.

Finally, the United States Department of the Navy's Core Values Charter defines the expected behavior of its members in the areas of "Honor, Courage, and Commitment". This listing may be helpful in understanding what honor means.

Department of the Navy
CORE VALUES CHARTER
HONOR

I am accountable for my professional and personal behavior. I will be mindful of the privilege I have to serve my fellow Americans. I will:

- Abide by an uncompromising code of integrity taking full responsibility for my actions and keeping my word.
- Conduct myself in the highest ethical manner in relationships with seniors, peers and subordinates.

- Be honest and truthful in my dealings within and outside the Department of the Navy.
- Make honest recommendations to my seniors and peers and seek honest recommendations from junior personnel.
- Encourage new ideas and deliver bad news forthrightly.
- Fulfill my legal and ethical responsibilities in my public and personal life.

Chapter 13

Character as Commitment

"The quality of a person's life is in direct proportion to
their commitment to excellence, regardless of their
chosen field of endeavor."
~ Vince Lombardi[28]

What integrity invites is nothing less than a personal commitment to life; a commitment freely given to discover the fullness, vitality, honor, and joy of living an excellent life. To do less is to resign yourself to a diminished life; failing to become what you ought to be, to discover the best inside you, and failing to reach your inborn potential.

To live the life of integrity requires that you take control of your life and commit yourself to developing your potential and unique gifts. Make no mistake, it will not be easy. Nothing of value in life is cheap. Beware that the moment you commit yourself to a life of integrity, obstacles will surely appear; tempting you to settle for second-best. Unfortunately, these obstacles may come from those closest to you; your family, friends and co-workers. The greatest obstacle, however, may be in your own mind; an inner voice saying "You cannot do that", "That will be too difficult", or "Who do you think you are?"

That last question is paramount: "Who DO you think you are?" If you know in your inner being that you are a person of worth with unlimited potential, then you owe it to yourself and others to commit to living the truly best life you can live. That is a life of integrity.

The Twenty-Mile Principle (Each Day, Every Day)

One of the best guidelines for reaching your goal of integrity is "The Twenty-Mile Principle". Jim Collins[3], author of the best-selling books *Built to Last*, and *Good to Great*, illustrated the importance to commitment and consistency in the 1911 race to the South Pole. Collins compared the strategies of Norwegian explorer Roald Amundsen and Robert Scott of the Royal Navy. Amundsen reached the South Pole five weeks ahead of Scott and led his party safely back to its ship within one day of its schedule, while Scott and his whole team perished in the snow and ice.

What made the critical difference? Scott's party would camp during blizzards and try to make up lost mileage on better days, while Amundsen committed to covering 20 miles every day, no less, regardless of the conditions. This "Twenty-Mile Principle" meant Amundsen's team was always moving toward their goal. Scott's expedition failed because they waited for favorable conditions. Sure, they might cover forty miles on a good day, but were idle many days waiting for better conditions.

Too often, you get caught between periods of significant accomplishments and days of idleness waiting for better circumstances. Commit yourself to start your quest for integrity today, and make sure you are moving toward your goal each day, every day, whether circumstances are favorable or not. Commitment helps overcome spikes of overachieving and idleness, and ensures you are moving toward your goal each day, every day; even if in only small steps. Accomplish monumental tasks by breaking them down into a series of smaller steps. If you accomplish one or more of the smaller steps every day, you will reach your goal eventually. Each day you will experience motivation by knowing that you are closer to your destination than you were the day before.

The Tortoise and the Hare

The old fable of the tortoise and the hare illustrates the importance of commitment and persistence. No doubt, a rabbit can cover a greater distance and in a much shorter time than a turtle. The rabbit has natural attributes for speed. Yet, in the fable, the turtle won the race because:

- The turtle ran the race. You cannot win a race if you are not in it.
- The turtle believed winning was possible. The odds were not good, but the turtle believed it was possible.
- The turtle was committed and consistent. Unlike the rabbit, the turtle made consistent progress toward the goal line.
- The turtle "kept on, keeping on". In spite of ridicule from the rabbit, the turtle kept the faith and finished the course.
- The turtle won. Honor and integrity accrue to those who build a strong character.

So, get in the race for integrity. Believe you can reach it. Make steady progress every day. Finish your course. Win your race for integrity.

Strength of character
Just as building a strong body requires exercise, building a strong character requires a similar commitment. The athlete disciplines self to overcome such obstacles as laziness, poor diet, and pain. My wife always said that if she waited until she felt "good enough" to go to work, she would never get there. Nevertheless, she got up every day and went to work and gave it 100% whether she felt like it or not. Recently she retired from the Federal government after nearly 45 years with two years of sick leave unused. To quote her, "A professional is someone who does a good job, whether they feel like it or not." Half the battle is just showing up and committing yourself to give the best you have to give.

Likewise, to have a strong character you must master the impulses that distract from reaching your goal of integrity.

- You must commit your whole self, including mind, heart, and soul; not just parts of yourself.
- You must overcome your doubts and fears of not being and becoming who you were meant to be. Have courageous character.
- You must master your emotions, for they are the most potent enemies of strong character.
- You must commit yourself to resist the temptations to get rich quick, take the easy way, and cut corners.

- You must fight daily against the onslaught of compromises to your integrity, especially those that appeal to your pride, pleasures, and promise you power.
- You must commit to being your genuine self, and not play roles or games with yourself and others that deny your authentic being.
- You must make sure that your word is your bond, that you honor your commitments and obligations.
- You must resist the cancer of character: procrastination.
- You must commit random and anonymous acts of kindness, especially to those most in need, or who cannot help themselves.
- You must realize character is infectious; that those who see your commitment will be inspired to live their own life of integrity.

Whereas the athlete masters the body, the person of character must master the mind and will.

Commitment, but commitment to what?

- To living in accord with values and principles for living with integrity.
- To performing virtues.
- To embodying character.
- To seeing life as a whole, not fragments, where my character is the same in all aspects of life.

Dr. Panza and Dr. Adam Potthast[23] wrote, "If you want to be a virtuous person, you have to make a real commitment to it. Basically, you have to take on the constant work of shaping, reshaping, and pruning the character that you already have to make sure you participate in the right kinds of behaviors and as a result cultivate just the right habits of thinking and feeling. After doing so, the right habits can take root and the seeds of virtue will be formed. In a nutshell: being virtuous is a lifelong task, and it requires practice, practice, and more practice. Basically, you need to embrace two points. First, no quick way exists to develop a settled habit of character in a way that doesn't require constant practice and commitment. The second is the recognition that when you succeed in cultivating habits into your character, those habits will literally transform the ways in which you experience the world."[20]

Below is an example of a preamble to a personal code of character. The preamble addresses the commitments required to build strong character and attain integrity.

Example Preamble to My Code of Character

I place ultimate value on attaining and sustaining personal integrity. I acknowledge that integrity will require commitment, discipline, and considerable effort. Because I have high standards and expectations of myself, I commit myself to a course of excellence and honor.

To guide me in my life of integrity, I pledge and commit myself to:

1. Never forget life is a gift and be grateful for it each and every day.
2. Believe in and do what I know in my heart is right, just and good.
3. Value the relationships and things that are genuine, especially love of family.
4. Live a principled life.
5. Pursue and achieve noble ideals and goals with excellence.
6. Live my life with justice, wisdom, courage and self-control.
7. Be honest, trustworthy and disciplined in all my dealings.
8. Grow spiritually through faith, hope and charity.
9. Be the genuine me with pure motives and good habits.
10. Have moral fiber and courage of character.
11. Accept responsibility and accountability for my actions and life.
12. Live a life of wholeness, completeness, true happiness.

At the beginning of each week, I will reflect upon my character and integrity by reviewing my Code of Character. I will strive to have wholeness, completeness and consistency in how I think, what I do, why I do it, and who I am.

As noted before, the United States Department of the Navy's Core Values Charter defines expectations of its members in the areas of "Honor, Courage, and Commitment". This listing may be helpful in understanding what commitment means.

Department of the Navy
CORE VALUES CHARTER
COMMITMENT

The day-to-day duty of every man and woman in the Department of the Navy is to join together as a team to improve the quality of our work, our people and ourselves.
I will:

- Foster respect up and down the chain of command.
- Care for the professional, personal and spiritual well-being of my people.
- Show respect toward all people without regard to race, religion or gender.
- Always strive for positive change and personal improvement.
- Exhibit the highest degree of moral character, professional excellence, quality and competence in all that I do.

Conclusion
Commit yourself to your personal quest for character and integrity. Remember, a quest is full of adventure and discoveries. As you discover life, you discover yourself.

Chapter 14

Character as Leadership

> "The supreme quality for leadership is
> unquestionably integrity.
> Without it, no real success is possible,
> no matter whether it is on a section gang,
> a football field, in an army, or in an office."
> ~ Dwight D. Eisenhower[28]

What is it about certain people that make them strong leaders? What are the character qualities of leadership? A quick review: ethics are how you think (beliefs), virtues are what you do (actions), and character is why you do it (motives, habits). Character is the "moral fiber" that stands between ethics and our virtues, making sure we are consistent in what we say and what we do.

Increasingly, leading businesses and organizations are recognizing the importance of character in leadership. Character is no longer relegated to a nice-to-have personal quality; companies are realizing character in its leaders gives them a significant competitive advantage. Major universities, such as Harvard School of Business, now require Master of Business Administration students to take courses in ethics, character and integrity. Major corporations actively recruit candidates with strong moral character strengths. Those leaders have skills that go beyond making the business profitable. A person without character may do that, for a while. Leaders who are in touch with their own personal character allow the enterprise to achieve results beyond the bottom line, and increase the organization's value in the community and economy. Leaders without character will sooner or later destroy a company's hard earned brand and reputation.

We expect exemplary leaders to be strong in character. Sometimes, we get disappointed, and reminded that all in positions of authority are not necessarily principled leaders. For the purpose of distinguishing these qualities of leadership, we use "managers" to identify those who are in roles of leadership (but who may or may not actually be leaders), and "leaders" to identify those who are what they believe in, demonstrate consistency between their ethical values and actions, demonstrate positive qualities that inspire those they work with, and are respected for their character. That is not to say managers are not leaders. Some are; others are not. The distinguishing element is character.

Dr. Theodore Malloch wrote, leadership "is a quality contained potentially in all of us, a quality that can be developed and realized, so that each of us is able to lead himself to his goal. This means that the true leader is also a good follower: he is able to take and receive advice, to receive and offer help, to join with others without subduing or alienating them."[15]

Many studies identify the top character traits of leaders. You should not be surprised to find that most of these qualities are components of integrity. Some are virtues, others character traits.

Top Character Qualities of Leadership

Below you will find a list of the Top Character Qualities organized around "The ABC Model" in no particular order.

Virtue – Qualities of Actions

1. **Compassion:** Compassion is a virtue of Charity. Compassion has spiritual connotations, for it refers to showing concern for the suffering or welfare of others, and shows mercy to others. In business, compassion manifests itself when leaders make an effort to understand the needs of their employees and take steps to address those needs and concerns. In a reality television show, "Undercover Boss", the recurring theme is that the

Chief Executive Officer has little knowledge of the trials and tribulations of the line crew until he or she walks a mile in their shoes. In every story, the CEO comes away with more compassion for the rank-and-file, and in doing so, engenders compassion from the workers.

2. **Fairness:** Fairness is a virtue of Justice. Fairness is treating people equitably and in a just manner. Leaders do not show partiality or play favorites. Leaders play by the rules, and that means the same set of rules for everyone. Being fair require candor and frankness, but also respect.

3. **Optimism:** Optimism is a virtue of Hope. Optimism is not blind hope, but a firm confidence that the team can overcome every obstacle in reaching the goal. Numerous movies tell heartwarming stories of coaches who take over teams that have lost hope in themselves, and the coach turns the team into champions. Leaders know that if you do not believe in yourself, you will never succeed. Someone said of an outstanding college football coach, "He can take his team and beat yours. But, he can also take your team and beat his." That is leadership.

4. **Passion, Inspiration:** Passion and inspiration are virtues of Faith. A leader must "have soul" and be faithful to the organization, co-workers, and most importantly to self. Passion is energy, commitment and enthusiasm for being the best and doing the best job possible. It is incumbent upon leaders to instill passion and spirit among the members. A leader's passion inspires others or provides focus on excellence and motivates the entire organization. If leaders are not passionate about their job, their role, their goal, it is doubtful the rank and file will be passionate about their work.

5. **Personal Strength:** Personal strength is a virtue of Courage. Fear of the unknown does not constrain courage. Managerial courage includes the willingness to do what is right in the face of risk. With "risk," there is a possibility of failure or loss and no guarantee that everything will turn out well. Acting with courage may result in unpleasant experiences, yet it is a fundamental ingredient of leadership.

6. **Respectfulness:** Respectfulness is a virtue of Trust. Respect is an essential quality of leadership. Respect must flow from management to rank-and-file, and back again. Without respect, an organization becomes "a house divided against itself, which cannot stand".

7. **Self-discipline:** Self-discipline is a virtue of both Discipline and Temperance. Leaders with self-discipline are able to exercise proper control over their thoughts emotions and actions, not allowing ego and emotions to get in the way of taking appropriate action. A leader's self-discipline prepares him or her to persevere in the face of problems and adversity. That self-discipline inspires confidence that they may be counted upon to do the right thing. There is a measure of increased influence and authority that comes from self-discipline. Self-discipline requires the maturity to do what is needed, not always what is expedient.

8. **Truthfulness:** Truthfulness is a virtue of Honesty. Honesty is essential to leadership and character. People value working for leaders who are open and honest, who they may trust to be honest with them about the reality of their situation. Successful leaders know how to exercise discretion in how they use and disclose information. They do not violate confidences.

9. **Vision:** Vision is a virtue of Faith. A leader is one who points the way. A manager is one who organizes the personnel and resources to reach the goal. A leader thinks strategically. A manager thinks tactically. Success requires both, but "Where there is no vision, the people perish." (Proverbs 29:18). Vision is the strategic goal of an organization. Vision is where teamwork and cooperation come together. The leader cannot reach the goal by him/herself. Teamwork and cooperation are strategic advantages. Unfortunately, many corporations have an outdated organization that discourages teamwork, with "every man for himself" and "turf protection" syndromes. Leaders find ways to break through these barriers for the good of all.

10. **Wisdom:** Wisdom is a virtue of Prudence. Wisdom is the ability to make well-formed judgments drawn from your experience and knowledge to implement an effective

course of action. Wisdom supports the formation of major decisions. Wisdom is greater than knowledge; it is the ability to take information and knowledge to decide upon the proper, prudent and wise course of actions. Wisdom is a critical quality of leadership.

Character - Qualities of Being

11. **Humility, Selflessness:** Humility and selflessness are character traits that reveal who you are. Managers have high drive that stems from their competitive nature. Many managers find humility to be a weakness. Leaders understand that humility is not being a wimp, but the capacity to put the needs of others before self. In doing so, they earn respect and loyalty that allows them to become "a leader among men". Jesus washed the feet of his disciples, earning their love, respect and loyalty. These leaders practice "servant leadership" which includes committing to your workers as much as the bottom line. The guiding principle of servant leadership is to serve rather than to lead. It requires a large measure of humility and self-assurance to serve your workers, being a steward of their efforts. Confident leaders have a realistic sense of perspective, an acceptance of their strengths and weaknesses. It requires courage to admit mistakes, to take responsibility. Selflessness means putting the needs of others before your own.

12. **Loyalty:** Loyalty is a character trait revealing internal strength. In business, loyalty is the commitment to the strategic objectives of the company and being prepared to harness the minds of workers and company resources to achieve those objectives. Leaders who demonstrate organizational loyalty show a deep commitment to do whatever it takes to make a company great regardless of how hard the decisions or how difficult the tasks may be. As a component of character, loyalty is a commitment to the idea and ideals of the organization.

13. **Competence:** Competence is a quality of character that reveals the state of being well prepared and qualified to fulfill a role or task, possessing a comprehensive

knowledge of the subject matter. Leaders must be competent in order to garner the confidence of others, and have expertise that commands the respect of peers and colleagues.

"I have a dream that my four little children will one day live in a nation where they will not be judged by the color of their skin but by the content of their character."
~ Martin Luther King Jr.[28]

Chapter 15

Character as Your Moral Fiber

"What the statesman is most anxious to produce is a certain moral character in his fellow citizens, namely a disposition to virtue and the performance of virtuous actions."
~ Aristotle[30]

"Moral fiber" is a term that seems to have gone out of style. Character makes up the moral strands of fiber linking your beliefs and actions, your ethics and virtues. Another name for moral fiber is moral courage; the consistent ability to hold to your ethics and virtues, even when circumstances change, or when expediency tempts you to "cut corners" with your integrity.

A study at the University of Toronto published in Psychological Science, a journal of the Association of Psychological Science, tested the difference between moral forecasting (how subjects predicted their behavior) and their moral actions (how subjects behaved), and the reasons behind mismatches. The study found the missing link between moral reasoning and moral action was emotions (fear, guilt, love), all of which play a central role in thinking and behavior, especially moral behavior. When people contemplate how they will act, they do not consider the intensity of the emotions they will feel at the time. The study illustrates how important moral fiber is to overcome such variables as emotions, feelings, temptations, expediency, or popular opinion, all of which may compromise your integrity.[27]

In another study published in the journal American Sociological Review, Jan E. Stets of UC Riverside and Michael J. Carter of CSU Northridge[27] found stock brokers, investment advisors, and mortgage lenders who caused the Great Recession that began in 2007 were able to act as they did, without shame or guilt, because their moral identity standard was set at a low level, and behavior that followed from their personal standard went unchallenged by their colleagues. Carter concluded, "One's identity standard guides a person's behavior. Then the person sees the reactions of others to one's own behavior. If others have a low moral identity and others do not challenge the illicit behavior that follows from it, then the person will continue to do what s/he is doing. This is how immoral practices can emerge."[27] Stets and Carter concluded studying the moral self is opportune given the unregulated practices of stock brokers, investment advisors, and mortgage lenders whose behavior facilitated the Great Recession in the United States. "The cost of their irresponsible practices has touched the lives of many innocent victims, as witnessed in the loss of individuals' retirement savings, homes, and jobs. The fact that a few greedy actors have the potential to damage the lives of many (as evidenced in the Bernie Madoff case) brings issues of right and wrong, good and bad, and just and unjust to public awareness," they said. "To understand the illicit behavior of some, we need to study the moral dimension of the self and what makes some individuals more dishonest than others."[27]

Christian Bovee, a 19th century author, said, "All men are alike in their lower natures; it is in their higher characters that they differ. What separates those who achieve integrity in life and those who do not is their "higher character" or moral fiber".[28]

Not only does it require moral fiber to hold to your own integrity, it requires an added dimension of moral courage to stand up to the unethical behavior of colleagues and others. A person with the highest character will strive for excellence, not settling for just the okay or acceptable. Helen Keller said, "Character cannot be developed in ease and quiet. Only through experiences of trial and suffering can the soul be strengthened, vision cleared, ambition inspired and success achieved."[28]

If you are playing with moral dynamite, CUT IT OUT...NOW! If you are treating your integrity lightly, I suggest you give it as much attention as your health and 401(k). If you have a good name, cherish it, guard it, and teach your friends and loved ones to live lives of integrity. Or, as John Wesley would say, "Live lives of holiness". I'm not calling for perfection. I am calling for a serious assessment of your personal integrity (or lack thereof) and honest efforts to establish and build lives of integrity. "For what does it profit a person to gain the whole world, and in the process lose one's soul?" (Mark 8:36)

Section Four

Integrity: Who You Are

"You are in integrity when the life you are living on the
outside matches who you are on the inside."
~ Alan Cohen[25]

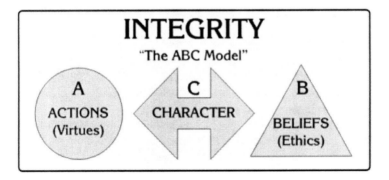

The story of integrity is as old as mankind, who has confronted the nature of integrity from the very beginning. Beginning with the story of the Garden of Eden, mankind has struggled with such issues as rules, boundaries, relationships, justice, honesty and integrity. The Greek philosophers addressed components related to values, ethics, virtues and character. Clearly they were struggling to articulate the same concept of integrity we are struggling to understand and realize today. Their reasoning is invaluable to understanding this subject.

The word integrity comes from the Latin term for wholeness, completeness, coherence, rightness, or purity. Integrity is consistency between word and deed. It implies the values expressed by words and those expressed through action will be consistent. The word integrity is the term most used in corporate mission statements. Almost every political candidate lays claim to integrity. Hypocrisy is the opposite of integrity.

What integrity is and is not

Merriam-Webster Dictionary[26] defines integrity as:

- Firm adherence to a code of values, especially moral or artistic: incorruptibility
- An unimpaired condition: soundness
- The quality or state of being complete or undivided: completeness

Integrity is a system of these interconnecting and interrelating components, including a person's consistency in beliefs, values, principles, ideals, ethics, actions, virtues and character. Integrity implies that a person has all, not just some or parts of these components. As such, integrity may be thought of as an entire system or framework for understanding and achieving an optimal life. Aristotle called the optimal life happiness; Jesus, in the Sermon on the Mount, referred to it as blessed (The Beatitudes); Buddha called it nirvana; and so on.

Integrity begins with a solid ethical structure which includes beliefs, values, principles and ideals. But having a good ethical structure is insufficient; you must live out those ethics through virtues. The degree to which you express virtues in harmony with your ethics defines your character. Character also reflects the authenticity and motivation of your virtues; including doing the right thing, at the right time, in the right way, for the right reason. Integrity is, therefore, the wholeness and consistency of your ethics, virtues and character; the opposite of which is discord, fragmentation and incompleteness. Those who possess integrity have developed into people whose thoughts, words and actions are consistent, reflecting an inner harmony.

A person has integrity to the extent that person's belief structure (ethics) and actions (virtues) originate from the same core group of belief, values, principles and ideals. While seeking an understanding of what integrity is, it may be helpful to state what integrity is not.

Perfection

First, integrity is not perfection. Perfection is the state of being free of faults or failings. Integrity is the state of being consistent in beliefs and actions, and complete in virtue. If individuals make a single mistake at some point in their lifetime, that blemish disqualifies them from the state of perfection but not necessarily from integrity. However, you should not assume that since human perfection seems impossible, the quest for integrity is equally futile. This argument leads to the conclusion that if a person does not possess integrity, he or she may work to improve upon their level of integrity, and potentially achieve integrity.

A Destination

Secondly, integrity is not "a destination". Rather, integrity should be viewed as a lifelong journey; or a way of life. For example, learning should not stop when you earn a diploma or degree. In much the same way, while you may reach milestones leading to integrity, you should continually develop your integrity throughout life. This argument may discourage some from beginning the journey. However, rather than seeing the quest for integrity as a never ending marathon, those who achieve integrity see the ever expanding benefits and qualities that accrue to those who continually improve upon their integrity.

Ethics

Thirdly, integrity is not "ethics". Ethics are internal beliefs and values, are subjective and may not be visible or measurable to others. Integrity involves translating your ethics into actions and deeds, or virtues. These virtues are objective; having been validated by social norms and expectations. The living out of these virtues may be observed in the shape of a person's character; the totality of which is tantamount to integrity. This argument illustrates why "ethics training" often fails to achieve its objectives. Ethics deals with the rules. Learning the rules, while an important step, does not get at the root of the issue. "The ABC Model" slogan is: "Ethics are how you think...virtues are what you do... character is why you do it...integrity is who you are".

Every parent faces this dilemma. Teach a child the rules, and you will soon discover the child has a way of exploring the boundaries of those rules ("But what if...?") so that they violate the spirit of the law without violating the letter of the law. Adults do the same thing. Politicians exposed in scandals frequently seek to justify their behavior by defining why it did not violate the letter of the law.

Another analogy comes from the popular cable series, "The Dog Whisperer". Cesar Millan has an extraordinary ability to correct the unruly behavior of dogs in a matter of seconds where the dog owners have failed in their efforts for years. How does he do it? Cesar does not focus on the symptoms (what the dog does), but gets to the root of who the dog is. Cesar rehabilitates dogs by teaching they are a member of the pack, not the pack leader, thereby changing their role, behavior, and who they are. Likewise, where ethics address the key issue of what a person thinks and how that impacts behavior, integrity gets to the deeper issue of who a person is; and how beliefs, values, ethics, virtues and character all work together to form integrity.

Morality

Integrity is not simply morality. While morality and integrity are closely intertwined, morality may be defined by "thou shalt not", or doing nothing. Integrity demands "thou shalt" do virtue ethics. A person who has never committed murder, stolen from others, or committed fraud may be moral to one degree. While admirable, the same person may not possess the wholeness and happiness that accrue to persons with integrity.

Why your integrity is important

Integrity is crucial for many reasons. Since integrity implies wholeness, it means that integrity touches every aspect of your life. For example, integrity impacts personal relationships, finances, spirituality, workplace, sports, recreation, academics, and politics, just to name a few. Integrity is crucial because it has the potential to enhance every aspect of living. Conversely, without integrity, having a whole, fulfilled and successful life is not likely. Integrity is what separates a successful organization from an unsuccessful one, and what separates excellence from the ordinary in individuals.

Why strive for integrity?

Ultimately, everyone is striving for success and happiness. Few find either, much less, both of these ideals. The common denominator between true happiness and honorable success is integrity; without which you will never achieve these desirable goals. A person with integrity "will", not "may", achieve success! Therefore, integrity should be a serious consideration for every person, family, organization and society.

The age old question, "Am I my brother's keeper?" applies to your motivation for integrity. First, as we learned in the financial scandals of 2008, one person's lack of integrity may bring down a career, family, company, and even a nation. The idea that one person without integrity may behave with impunity is a myth because of the potential far-reaching consequences. No matter how small the action, everything you do and the way in which you do it has consequences to you and others.

Secondly, you have a responsibility to your children and future generations to provide the tools for understanding and achieving integrity in an ever changing world. One generation removed from those who value and practice integrity may not have the knowledge and skills to establish their own. For example, a third or fourth generation of "absentee father" family units establishes a norm. Many of those living in that norm have no frame of reference for both fathers and mothers taking full responsibility for their children's care, education and well-being. Conversely, examples and role models reinforce integrity.

Thirdly, you get your cues of what integrity is from your family (parents and grandparents, aunts and uncles) and society (especially what we see in the media). For the most part, we have failed in both these areas. We are becoming farther removed from the era when honor and responsibility were core values of our society. Society is increasingly distancing itself from integrity. In the 1950s, students received grades on citizenship which included integrity. We no longer consider that a part of education – more often the media portrays lying and cheating as the way to succeed. You only have to watch one episode of "Survivor" or "The Bachelor" to see this illustrated. If your societal values are being established by television reality shows, then you are learning that lying, cheating and stealing are the way to success.

How you may attain or improve integrity

As we noted earlier, integrity stems from the Latin: integer (whole, complete). In mathematics, an integer is a "whole number"; such as 7, as opposed to a factionalized number (7/1), or a "real number" (7.0). In this context, integrity encompasses the inner sense of "wholeness" derived from consistency of character. As such, people "have integrity" to the extent that they behave according to the values, beliefs and principles they claim to hold.

In the context of behavior and morality, integrity may be seen as basing your actions on an internally-consistent framework of principles. You may describe a person as having integrity to the extent that everything that person does or believes — actions, methods, measures and principles —stem from the same core group of values.

In the context of accountability, integrity is a measure of consistency between your actions and your principles. Your value system materializes as a set of values and measures that are consistent with expectations.

Hypocrisy is when one part of a value system is evidently at odds with another, demanding a reconciliation of the conflict between values or beliefs and actions to develop internal consistency.

Chapter 16

Your Personal Integrity and Rewards

"A person of integrity lurks somewhere inside each of us:
a person we feel we can trust to do right, to play by the
rules, to keep commitments."
~ Stephen L. Carter[1]

Integrity impacts your life at a truly basic level. The essential
fact is that no one can give integrity to you. You cannot inherit
it, and you certainly cannot buy it. Integrity is like the pearl of great
price, the treasure hidden in the field, the leaven that causes the
whole loaf of bread to rise. (Matthew 13). It is that for which many
respectable people have spent a lifetime searching, and once
they find it, they sell all they have to obtain it. Again, you cannot
buy integrity, but its value is beyond measure.

Look at the following characterizations of a person with and
without integrity. Integrity for an individual includes:

- Your character and trustworthiness
- How others perceive you as a person
- How you honestly feel about yourself
- Your beliefs, values, principles and ideals (ethics)
- How you live out your life through virtues

A person with integrity is:

- Courageous
- Disciplined
- Fair, just
- Happy
- Honest
- Honorable
- Successful
- Trustworthy
- Whole, complete
- Wise

Without integrity, a person frequently is:

- Corruptible – more easily "cheats"
- Fragmented – unfocused, incomplete
- Hypocritical – says one thing, does another
- Incapable of sincere relationships with self and others
- Lacking self esteem
- Unreliable – unpredictable, inconsistent
- Untrustworthy – lacking defined moral core

If your self-perception is that of a person with questionable or inadequate values, you will not feel positive about yourself. Consequently you cannot achieve happiness in your life and relationships, nor will you achieve the full potential you are capable of achieving. A single person deeply lacking integrity and morals is like cancer, negatively influencing the people around them until they have created a culture of untrustworthiness or greed, which can undermine and even destroy an entire organization or business.

The life of integrity is like that of the warrior-soldier. D. Joseph Jacques[10] in *Chivalry-Now* identified the qualities of such a life:

- An intensity for life filled with the energy and readiness to act when needed.
- A desire to perfect one's self for the benefit of others.
- A determination to protect one's family, neighborhood, nation and world.

- Doing one's best in everything.
- Being true to oneself and to others.
- Honesty. Loyalty. Integrity.
- Fairness and the willingness to stand up for what is right, even when everyone is against you.
- Idealism joined with reality.
- A sense of duty greater than one's own needs.

Be ONE! Be a person of integrity.

We now turn attention to the benefits that naturally accrue to a person of integrity. While these are worthy and desirable qualities of life, you should see each as a by-product of integrity rather than a stand-alone goal to reach. By striving for integrity, you will (not "may") realize wholeness, completeness, happiness, success, wisdom, abundance and peace.

1. Your Wholeness

"The presence of a noble nature, generous in its wishes,
ardent in its charity, changes the lights for us: we begin
to see things again in their larger, quieter masses, and
to believe that we too can be seen and judged in the
wholeness of our character."
~ George Eliot[28]

The first reward of integrity is wholeness or completeness. The term "integrity" has the same root as "whole". Steven Carter said, "Integrity, as applied to a person, carries more than a sense of wholeness, because a person must have something to be whole about."[1]

Wholeness means the opposite of fragmented; a wholeness that is undivided. It is an extremely elusive quality. Integrity is having your heart, mind and willpower all united, or unified. Abraham Lincoln knew this when he quoted the Bible text, "And if a house be divided against itself, that house cannot stand." (Mark 3:25) A divided nation has no integrity, and neither does a divided person. A hypocrite is a divided and inauthentic person.

The whole human being means focusing all aspects of yourself; mentally, spiritually, and physically. In this context, integrity is the inner sense of "wholeness" deriving from qualities such as honesty and consistency of character. As such, you may judge that others "have integrity" to the extent that they act according to the values, beliefs and principles they claim to hold.

Getting to know you

Ronald Greer's book[9] *If You Know Who You Are, You'll Know What To Do*, is in two parts. The first part is "Personal Integrity: A Life of Wholeness". Greer says that having integrity first requires discovering who you are. That process involves asking yourself, "What do I value?", "What do I believe?", and "What is important and/or sacred to me?" Integrity involves discerning your core, your spiritual center. It takes time to get to know you so that when something happens, you can listen to your heart and know what it is you genuinely believe and how you should act.

Greer defines sin as "being separated from God and being estranged from who we are." This fragmentation of self includes:

- Self-esteem: "sin is when we think we are less than we are ..."
- Narcissism: "sin is when we think we are greater than we are..."
- Drifting: "sin is when we think we are anything other than who we are ..."

If you are one person at work, another person at home, and yet another person in your leisure, you are fragmented, not whole, and certainly not a person of integrity.

2. Your Completeness

"When you come together with your other half,
you immediately experience a sense of wholeness
and completeness."
~ Andrew Cohen[28]

As we have noted, the word "integrity" stems from the Latin adjective, integer (whole, complete). Wholeness and completeness are not the same thing in the context of integrity, although they are two sides on the coin.

- To be whole is to be unified, with singleness in purpose and being.
- To be complete means not lacking in any virtue. Nothing is missing.

Another way to express the difference is that the complete person has all the parts, and the whole person has all the parts organized. Think of opening a new puzzle and pouring all the pieces on a table. You assume all the pieces are there. If so, it is a complete puzzle; but it is not yet whole. You cannot make out the whole image from the pieces. After you put all the pieces in their proper place, you see a single, united "whole" image.

As I have struggled with understanding integrity, the puzzle metaphor has come up repeatedly. The major pieces to the puzzle are actions, beliefs and character (ABC). But each of these components have their own pieces, including the four parts of ethics, the 10 primary virtues, and the moral fibers of character. I love working with puzzles. It relaxes me as nothing else. Recently, my wife gave me an unusual puzzle; a topographical map of the five mile radius around my family home in Mississippi. It was one of the most difficult and yet treasured puzzles I have ever completed. Because the terrain around Yazoo City is flat land, there were few obvious clues for how each puzzle piece related. I struggled to match piece to piece, and finally neared completion. To my horror, I discovered that the last piece was missing. We launched an all-out search, almost turning the house upside down in search of the missing piece. Finally, I spotted the prodigal piece on the floor. Somehow, it had fallen into my pants cuff, and tried to escape.

To be whole and complete is much like that puzzle. To have integrity, there must be all the pieces, and they must all be in their place, supporting the integrity and character of the puzzle. The quest for integrity is the task of putting all the pieces of the puzzle together, which requires that you have all the pieces and that they unite to reveal one character or image.

3. Your Happiness

"Happiness for a reason is just another form of misery because
the reason can be taken away from us at any time."
~ Deepak Chopra[2]

Aristotle said that happiness (eudaimonia) is the ultimate goal
of virtue-ethics. Thousands of books (including this one) attempt
to define, clarify and understand what this means.

True happiness is the universal goal of human life. Ask a
dozen people what produces happiness, and you will probably
get such responses as:

- Money and riches
- Fame and popularity
- Power and influence
- Beauty and sex
- Pleasure and leisure
- Independence
- A life of no responsibilities

Dr. Malloch stated it this way, "happiness (eudaimonia) is 'an
activity of the soul in accordance with virtue.' This definition is as
valid today as when Aristotle first presented it as a cornerstone of
his ethical theory, though it goes quite again the teachings of the
modern 'happiness experts,' whose attempts to measure happiness actually reduce it to a succession of momentary pleasures."[15]

Happiness is not the same as laughter or amusement. Many
comedians, who make everyone else laugh, have unhappy lives
themselves. Happiness has many disguises and decoys. Most
epic stories and Greek tragedies tell the heartbreak that results
from chasing illusive happiness. How sad it is to see someone
waste their life in pursuit of happiness, never to find it. Genuine
happiness lies in deeds that lead to virtue, not just amusements
and pleasures.

A recent study at the University of Zurich found anyone who
trains character strengths increases their sense of wellbeing. It
proved for the first time that this kind of "character training" works.
The study found character strengths and their connection with

wellbeing are important, discovering what makes life most worth living, what constitutes life satisfaction.[27]

The irony is that happiness is the by-product of character and integrity. It is not a commodity you can buy or obtain in any other way. Counselors know from experience that many people are unhappy because they expect their spouse, children, or employer to "make them happy". No person or thing can make you happy. You are the only one who can make you happy. That can only happen when you have inner wholeness, peace, and integrity.

4. Your Peace

"Each one has to find his peace from within.
And peace to be real must be unaffected by outside circumstances."
~ Mohandas K Gandhi[28]

Peace is not just the lack of conflict and violence. Inner peace is being at peace, mentally and spiritually, even in the face of discord or stress. Being at peace is when there is a healthy balance and harmony in life; the opposite of stress and anxiety. Peace is essential for happiness. Peace of mind, serenity, and calmness are descriptions of a disposition free from the effects of stress.

Plato argued that virtues are states of the soul. The just person's soul is harmonious, with all its parts functioning properly. By contrast, Plato stated the unjust man's soul, without virtues, is chaotic and at war with itself. Even if he were able to satisfy his desires, the lack of inner harmony and unity spoil any chance of achieving peace and happiness. Inner peace comes in the spiritual part of human life. Prayer and meditation are means to find peace in the world's leading religions. Jesus Christ said, "Peace I leave with you, my peace I give unto you: not as the world gives, give I unto you. Let not your heart be troubled, neither let it be afraid." (John 14:27). He also said, "Come to me, all you who labor and are burdened, and I will give you rest. Take my yoke upon you and learn from me, for I am meek and humble of heart; and you will find rest for your souls. For my yoke is easy, and my burden light." (Matthew 11:28-30).

Worldly peace is extremely temporal and may disappear in a moment. Genuine peace emerges from the inner soul, where the winds and storms of life cannot destroy or steal peace. No one can take your peace from you without you allowing them to do so. Mahatma Gandhi confirmed, "Each one has to find his peace from within. And peace to be real must be unaffected by outside circumstances."[28] Gandhi makes an important observation when he said genuine peace is independent of "outside circumstances". That is how some people are able to remain calm and productive when it seems the foundations of the universe are crumbling around them.

Nothing can bring you peace but yourself. Only through integrity is it possible to know true inner peace.

5. Your Success

"Success comes from knowing that you did your best to
become the best that you are capable of becoming."
~ John Wooden[28]

Every young person setting out in life wonders, "How can I
live a successful life?" It all depends on how you define success.
In order to obtain success, you must have goals or objectives for
your life. Success does not equal wealth, fame or power.

According to Nicomachean Ethics, there are three reasons
for living.

- First, enjoying pleasures
- Second, earn a respectable name for yourself in your eyes
  and the eyes of the community, such as a career in public
  service.
- Third, understand and appreciate the universe, such as a
  philosopher.

Everyone defines success for their life in their own way. A
well-lived life is the best possible "good" for you to succeed as a
human being through virtuous living under the guidance your soul.
Since success is a perfect and self-sufficient objective, worthy of
pursuit for itself, it must include the whole of life and all the most
eminent virtues. Success in life, the best possible good for man, is
therefore, living one's whole life in a rational way under the guidance of the best virtues of the rational soul.

Dr. Malloch said, "We prepare for success by acquiring virtues
– dispositions that help us to take risks, to make decisions, to take
responsibility for our actions, and to accept wise advice. These
virtues are the most important part of our human capital."[15] My personal motto for successful living is: "Be kind. Be just. Be blessed."
The Greek word for "happy" (makarios) translates into English as
"blessed", which connects us with the Divine.

The question is never about whether a person of integrity will
be successful. The life of integrity guarantees success in living.
That does not means you will become a millionaire, a movie star,
or invent the next best thing. It does mean, without question, you

163

will be successful in living, for you have your priorities in order, and your values at work.

Wherever your road of life carries you, you will travel with success.

6. Your Abundance

"I have come that you might have life abundantly"
~ Jesus

Growing up with a family of nine in a four room shack in rural Mississippi, we learned some basic lessons about scarcity and abundance. While many from the outside may have thought we had nothing of value, we knew we had an abundance of almost everything; especially love, faith and hope for a better tomorrow. When David Roberts, my best buddy, came over to spend the night, Mother would just add some water to the soup and set another plate. And sleeping five boys in one room is not much more difficult than four. We had plenty to eat with chickens, hogs and vegetables all around. There were fish in the creek, wildlife in the woods, and wild berries and fruit ready for the picking.

Today's news warns how we are running out of water, clean air, and the basics for survival. I do not discount those warnings. Abundance is all around us; especially the abundance of opportunity.

In the 2011 book, *Abundance: The Future is Better Than You Think*, Peter Diamandis[6] and Steven Kotler[12] turn the commonly held belief that the earth is running out of resources on its head. Rather than perpetuate the fear that the world is dying a slow death, and the population bomb that will place ten billion people on the planet by 2050, Diamandis and Kotler offer examples of how the world's scarcity can be turned into abundance. The book is fascinating, and full of optimism not easily seen in today's media. It is not a "feel good" book, but a well-thought-out rationale for how we may deal with the problems of scarcity in the years to come. Simply stated, Diamandis and Kotler espouse the notion that rather than a planet running out of resources, there is reasoned hope (with the right combination of technology, entrepreneurs and human ingenuity) for solving almost every problem confronting us.

"Imagine a world of nine billion people with clean water, nutritious food, affordable housing, personalized education, top-tier medical care, and nonpolluting, ubiquitous energy. Building this better world is humanity's greatest challenge. What follows is the story of how we can rise to meet it." Diamandis and Kotler write from a secular viewpoint, and admit that there will be catastrophes, wars, and famines. But as I read, my soul resounded that all is not doom and gloom. There are incredible opportunities: a solution for almost every scarcity.

We actually live in a different world than just a few decades ago. For example, while there was just one computer on campus at Delta State when I attended (and they did not let students touch it), in the recent past, a couple college students created Facebook in their dorm room and started a revolution in how billions of people order their daily lives. We now have more information at our fingertips today than the President had a decade ago.

Diamandis offers a "pyramid of abundance". There are three levels: the lowest belonging to the needs of food, water, shelter and so on. The middle tier identifies the catalysts for growth; such as education, communications and information. The top level, where scarcity gets translated into abundance, are freedom and health, the prerequisites enabling an individual to contribute to society. You do not have to be a major corporation or a national government to change the world. Anyone with common sense and a vision of how to turn scarcity into abundance can change the world...TODAY.

Taking Diamandis' premise that abundance is right before our eyes, I translate the analogy into the kind of abundant living that the Greek philosophers said was the result of living with integrity. When most people hear abundance, they automatically see dollar signs. We easily equate abundance, the good life, with material possessions, or things only money can buy. That is not what abundance means in this context. The kind of abundance integrity provides comes from "the well of living waters that will never run dry" that Jesus described to the woman at the well. This abundance is the wealth of inner resources that money cannot purchase.

7. Your Wisdom

"Knowledge comes, but wisdom lingers."
Alfred Lord Tennyson[28]

Philosophy ("philo" love and "sophia" wisdom) literally means "the love of wisdom". Aristotle defined wisdom as the understanding of causes, knowing why things are a certain way, rather than merely knowing that things are a certain way.

Dr. Deepak Chopra[2] made a fundamental distinction between knowledge and wisdom in his dialogue with Dr. Leonard Mlodinow[18].

- Science is about knowledge.
- Spirituality is about wisdom.

Deepak went so far as to say science will never be able to attain wisdom, although science has and will continue to accumulate vast amounts of knowledge. The reason being: there is a spiritual dimension to wisdom that science excludes.

For the record, this author is all in favor of science and spirituality, knowledge and wisdom.

A basic definition of wisdom is making use of knowledge. The opposite of wisdom is folly and foolishness. Wisdom is a deep understanding that results in the ability to apply perceptions, judgments and actions in keeping with this understanding. It requires control of your emotions. Wisdom is also an understanding what is true. Wisdom includes discernment and insight.

Confucius said, "By three methods we may learn wisdom: First, by reflection, which is noblest; second, by imitation, which is easiest; and third by experience, which is the bitterest."[28]

Prudence, which is the virtue related to wisdom, is one of the four cardinal virtues. A life of integrity has wisdom as its hallmark.

Chapter 17

Your Professional Integrity

"Real integrity is doing the right thing,
knowing that nobody's going to know
whether you did it or not."
~ Oprah Winfrey[28]

While we hope we learned lessons from the scandals of the early 2000s (Enron, WorldCom, the financial collapse of 2008, the Madoff Ponzi scheme, etc.) a recent survey offers the following disturbing findings:

- 76 percent of MBA graduates reported they were willing to commit fraud to enhance profit reports to management, investors, and the public;
- Fewer than 50 percent of employees believe their employers have high ethical integrity;
- 30 percent of all employees report that they "know or suspect ethical violations such as falsifying records, unfair treatment of employees, and lying to top management;"
- 41 percent of employees in the private sector and 57 percent of employees in the public/government sector are aware of ethical misconduct or illegal activities;
- 60 percent of employees state that they know but have not reported instances of misconduct in their organizations. Most employees cite the lack of companies' confidentiality policies as reasons for not coming forward about ethical

misconduct. They fear "whistle-blower" retaliation and that existing policies will not protect them.

In the meantime, the headlines reveal a steady stream of breakdowns in integrity that cost businesses billions in litigation, incalculable losses to reputation and brand image, lost sales and CEOs and CFOs sent to prison.

Dr. Robert C. Chandler of Pepperdine University said, "No company is immune from these threats. Prudent businesses must plan to manage integrity continuity by assessing their vulnerability to ethical disasters, taking proactive measures, and preparing their organizations to mitigate and survive when such scandals break." (Graziadio Business Review, "Avoiding Ethical Misconduct Disasters", Volume 8 Issue 3, 2005) Integrity for an organization includes how it operates internally and externally. Internally, integrity impacts how the organization treats its employees and how the employees conduct themselves. Externally, integrity involves how an organization treats its clients and vendors.

Integrity for an organization includes:

- Their reputation.
- Their trustworthiness and reliability.
- How they conduct business and treat customers, employees, and vendors.
- Their employee morale.
- Their probability for success.

Without integrity, an organization frequently is:

- Disreputable – has a bad reputation.
- Unreliable – unpredictable, inconsistent.
- Corrupt – does not conduct business honestly.
- Demoralized – employees are unmotivated, feel some colleagues get ahead by cheating.
- Untrustworthy – lacking defined moral core.
- At High Risk - greater chance of scandal, disgrace, liability.

For an organization, business or institution, 99 out of 100 employees or members may have integrity; but "one bad apple" can destroy the integrity of the whole group. Ultimately, the person lacking integrity will take a shortcut which may cause injury, lawsuit, or even death and can cause the entire organization to fail or suffer permanent damage. Benefits of integrity in an organization means a focus and renewal on achieving integrity can result in:

- Reduced risk
- Less waste
- Fraud abatement
- Less abuse
- More honesty
- Improved relationships
- Better productivity
- Higher morale
- Increased probability for success

Professional people exercise specialized knowledge and skills. How they use this knowledge is a moral issue called professional ethics. One of the earliest examples of professional ethics is the Hippocratic Oath to which medical doctors still adhere to this day. The problem with codes of ethics is that answers are not always black and white. There are, sometimes, grey areas where the answers are not so simple.

Professional organizations ethical standards include:

- Accountability
- Confidentiality
- Impartiality
- Obedience to the law
- Respect
- Transparency
- No Conflicts of Interest

The benefit of values for business

A study by professors at Bentley University found that among the benefits of a business value-based culture are:

- Increased awareness of ethical issues.
- Commitment to the organization.
- Employee honesty.
- Willingness to communicate openly about problems.

- Willingness to report an Ethics violation to management.
- Improved decision making.
- Willingness to seek advice about ethical issues.
- Reduced unethical conduct.

(Adapted from "Why Ethics Matter: A Business without values is a Business at Risk", by Dawn-Marie Driscoll and W. Michael Hoffman, akpsi.org, Autumn 2010)

How Personal and Professional Integrity Relate

Establishing your personal integrity is a profound undertaking. Relating personal and professional integrity presents an even greater challenge, if for no other reason it involves more people.

Your Integrity is "on the line"

Your boss asks you to alter the numbers in your monthly report to make sales look better than they actually were. At that moment, your personal integrity and your boss' lack of integrity come into conflict. Almost every day, in many circumstances, individuals find themselves facing similar challenges.

Professor Robert Solomon wrote "integrity is not itself a virtue so much as it is a synthesis of the virtues, working together to form a coherent whole. This is what we call...character."[24] When one has the "wholeness" of virtues, he or she is living with integrity.

Professional Integrity

"Professional" refers to anyone who earns a living; rather than a narrower context of professions, such as doctors, lawyers, teachers, and other professions. Professor Solomon adds, "The word integrity means "wholeness," wholeness of virtue, wholeness as a person, wholeness in the sense of being an integral part of something larger than the person—the community, the corporation, society, humanity, and the cosmos."[24]

Personal and professional integrity are dependent upon each other. In one sense, all integrity is personal. However, whereas individuals may discern their own set of ethics, an organization establishes its set of values, code of conduct, and policies in collaboration with stakeholders. Corporations rely upon humans to carry out their mission, survive, and succeed.

171

Corporate Culture and Integrity

All organizations develop rituals, traditions, procedures, formal and informal systems which form the "corporate culture". Corporate integrity is a manifestation of corporate culture, which ultimately stems from the actions of its individuals (employees, clients, vendors, supervisors, managers, owners and governing boards).

Likely, your personal integrity will sooner or later come in conflict with corporate culture and professional integrity.

Examples:

- Your supervisor asks you to "modify" your report so your whole department will qualify for a bonus or reward.
- A vendor presents you with a rather expensive "gift". The vendor is one of three vendors bidding on a large contract with your company.
- Your boss left for the day, and it is 30 minutes before 5:00. It is the day before a holiday, and the phone has not rung for an hour. Traffic is going to be terrible, and you certainly would like to get an early start to the holiday.

The Options

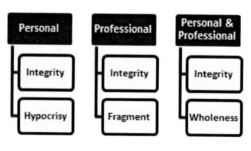

Figure A

Option 1

The first option is to seek personal integrity without consideration for professional integrity. The only way to begin the journey to integrity is to start with you. You must do the difficult work of thinking through your ethics, translating them into actions of virtue, and achieving the wholeness of character. The opposite of personal integrity is dishonesty, or hypocrisy (saying one thing and doing another).

Option 2

The second option is to live within two different systems: one, your personal integrity, and two, the system of integrity defined by your colleagues, company, or profession. When there are differences in these systems, the concept of wholeness is destroyed, making true integrity impossible. Living in two different worlds leads to fragmentation.

Option 3

The third option, relating personal and professional integrity, is the only way to living ideally. Doing so will not be easy. Integrity does not mean you may never compromise. Whenever personal and professional integrity come into conflict, an opportunity exists for both individuals and organizations to reevaluate what you do, why you do it, and how it impacts yourself and others. Integrity is dynamic and growing, not monolithic and static.

Risks and Courage

When you see something in the corporate culture that challenges integrity, the easy path is to do nothing. To confront the lack of integrity requires courage and comes with risks, including losing your job! That is why it is crucial to establish your personal integrity in a well thought out manner before attempting to relate it to professional or corporate integrity.

Some things to keep in mind when deciding if, how and when to deal with conflicts in personal and professional integrity are:

1. Unless the environment is corrupt, the organization will respect that an individual has the courage to take a stand. It is not just the individual's integrity at stake; the organization's integrity is also on the lin

2. Even when they disagree, most co-workers respect a person who values honor more than popularity.

3. Careful consideration must be given regarding to whom, how, when and in what setting one will deal with the conflicting points of integrity.

4. Determine ahead of time the risks, consequences, and potential outcomes. Is your personal integrity more valuable to you than the risks? If the answer is yes, then you will find the courage to confront the issue, and accept the outcome.

5. The decision you make is yours. Either way, you must live with the consequences. Seek counsel from someone you trust.

Summary

You do not live a life of integrity in isolation. Sooner or later, and more often than you would like, personal and professional integrity will come into conflict. Attempting to resolve the conflict by separating your personal and professional integrity destroys both. Integrity impacts every aspect of your life: your relationships, finances, politics, recreation, academics, and careers. You will never achieve integrity in any of these areas unless you start with personal integrity. Taking the considerable effort to establish personal integrity, and having the courage to relate personal and professional integrity is the only way to achieve "whole" integrity.

Chapter 18

Your Integrity Toolkit

"This celebration of integrity is intriguing: we seem to carry on a passionate love affair with a word that we scarcely pause to define."
~ Stephen L. Carter[1]

An artisan's best resource is the toolkit. Can you imagine a carpenter with no hammer or saw, a plumber with no wrench, or an artist with no brushes? To do their work, they all need the best tools, and so do you as the artisan of your life of integrity.

"The ABC Model" provides the following seven tools to help you design, plan and construct your integrity.

- **"The ABC Model"** – The Model itself is the foundation to understanding and achieving a life of integrity
- **Four Virtuous Norms** – Four questions to ask yourself when dealing with an ethical or moral dilemma
- **Integrity Quadrangle** – Four filters to help decide if your principles are consistent
- **Integrity Scorecard** – A resource to quantify and track your ethics, virtues, character traits, and integrity
- **Integrity LifeMap** – A step by step guide to help you get started toward a life of integrity
- **Values Calculator** – A method to help determine your values by ranking their importance to you

- **Personal Code of Character** – A comprehensive charter to document, plan, and navigate your life of integrity.

1. Your ABC Model

"The ABC Model" gives you the big picture of integrity. It illustrates how (A) Actions and virtues, (B) Beliefs and ethics, and (C) Character fit together to produce integrity.

"The ABC Model" illustrates that one component alone is not enough. Ethics by themselves are "faith without works". Virtues by themselves are simply "good deeds". It is only when ethics and virtues align through the agency of character, including pure motives and excellent habits, that the wholeness of integrity comes into focus.

The next time you hear someone say, "Integrity is honesty", you will be able to reply, "Not exactly! Honesty is an vital component of integrity, but honesty is a virtue." The next time your company sends you to "Ethics Training" you might ask, "When are we going to get some Integrity Training"? And if Human Resources says, "Ethics Training is Integrity Training", you may say, "Not exactly".

"The ABC Model" comes with a slogan that helps you visualize the model in its totality:

Ethics are how you think...

Virtues are what you do...

Character is why you do it...

Integrity is who you are!

By knowing what integrity is and is not, you have the best chance to attain the life of wholeness, completeness, happiness, peace, wisdom, abundance and success.

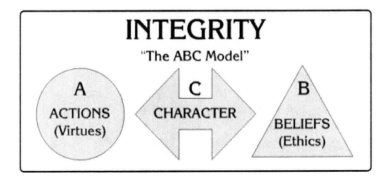

2. Your Four Virtuous Norms

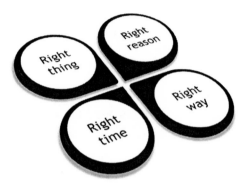

When confronted with an ethical dilemma, and you want to know what virtuous action you should take, you should ask yourself four basic questions.

Norm One: Is this the right thing to do?

It takes the virtue of courage to do the right thing, especially when it is unpopular or may cost something. Cowardice looks the other way and pretends there is no need to act. Do the right thing, because it is right!

Norm Two: Am I doing this for the right reason?

It takes the virtue of justice to do things for the right reason. This calls into play your motives and character.

Norm Three: Is this the right time to do it?

It takes the virtue of prudence to know when to act, and when not to act. Procrastination is an awful vice, and so is rashness, where "fools rush in". Remember, "Justice delayed is justice denied".

Norm Four: Am I doing it in the right way?

It takes the virtue of temperance to do things in the right way. Striving for excellence in all tasks, great and small, requires patience, persistence and doing it right the first time. Cutting corners and taking short cuts almost always comes back to hurt in the long run.

If the answer is "Yes" to all four questions, most likely you will be doing the virtuous thing, demonstrating the character of a person with integrity.

3. Your Integrity Quadrangle

The Reverend John Wesley, founder of Methodism, was a master of organization. His meticulous attention to details and organizational skills prompted his critics to brand him the "method-ist", the name by which millions of his followers today are known. Wesley formulated "The Wesleyan Quadrilateral"[31] as a tool for his followers to use in formulating their beliefs and practices. Church historians question whether Wesley actually codified the Quadrilateral into one system, but few argue he used these four questions in arriving at his beliefs. With credit to Mr. Wesley, we adapt the Quadrilateral as a filter through which you may refine your beliefs, values and principles.

When testing your ethics and virtues, as yourself four questions: "Is this ethic (belief) or virtue (action)…"

Filter One: In alignment with my authority?

This is the filter of legitimacy. First, you must decide what your authority is. For Wesley, it was The Bible. For the courts, it is the Constitution and laws. For a corporation, it is the body of policies and procedures. For you, it is your Code of Character, whether documented or not. If your ethics or virtues do not align with your authority, take time to identify the cause of the discrepancy.

Filter Two: Consistent with my past actions?

This is the filter of consistency. Wesley used "tradition" here, and asked his followers if their beliefs and actions were consistent with the traditions of the church. We modify Wesley's tradition, "Am I consistent in my beliefs and actions?" Throughout "The ABC Model" we have insisted that inconsistency between ethics and virtues makes integrity impossible. Where there is inconsistency, either the ethic or virtue must change to provide consistency of character, and wholeness of integrity.

Filter Three: Validated by my experience?

This is a filter of intuition. If someone suggests putting your hand on a hot stove, your experience will respond with that is not a smart idea. This intuitive response to the totality of your life experiences is valuable. If your employer, peers, or perceived authority request you to believe or do something that does not resonate with your experience, trust your intuition and investigate further before acting.

Filter Four: Reasonable?

This is the filter of common sense. For centuries, the world was flat and the center of the universe. As astronomers gathered more evidence, those premises became less reasonable. If your beliefs and actions do not pass the test of reason and common sense, you should revisit and reanalyze them.

4. Your Integrity Scorecard

The Integrity Scorecard is a resource to quantify and track your ethics, virtues, character traits, and integrity. Simply give yourself a score on each virtue on a scale of 0 to 5 with 0 being the poorest score.

First, give yourself a score on consistency between the virtue and your ethical system using the 0 to 5 scale. Next, give yourself a score on how well you exemplify the virtue in your actions and behavior using the 0 to 5 scale. The highest score for each virtue would be 5 + 5 = 10. The highest cumulative score for your Integrity Scorecard for all 10 virtues would be 100. When done, look at your self-assessment and note where you need to make improvements.

Review and retake the Scorecard periodically, perhaps once every three months. You will be able to chart and record your improvement or decline in each area of your character.

Virtues	How well do I rate the consistency of my actions with my beliefs, values, principles and ideals in this area of my life? (0-5)	How well do I rate myself on my actions and behavior in this area of my life? (0-5)	Total Column 2 plus Column 3
Justice			
Temperance			
Prudence			
Courage			
Honesty			
Trust			
Discipline			
Faith			
Hope			
Charity (love)			
Total			

5. Your Values Calculator

An excellent way to prioritize your list of values is to isolate the first two values on your list. Then ask yourself if you could have only one of the two, which would it be?

Here is an example list of values (listed alphabetically):

1. Balance in life
2. Benevolence
3. Devotion to family and/or friends
4. Fun & Joy
5. Genuine, authentic living
6. Happiness
7. Health and wholeness
8. Justice
9. Knowledge
10. Spirituality

Example

Round One:

Question: If I have to choose between (1) Balance in life, and (2) Benevolence, which one would I choose?

Answer: (1) Balance in life

Question: If I have to choose between (3) Devotion to family, and (4) Fun and Joy, which one would I choose?

Answer: (3) Devotion to family

And so on through the list. Then, conduct a second round prioritizing the ones you selected.

Round Two:

Question: If I have to choose between (1) Balance in life, and (3) Devotion to the family, which one would I choose?

Answer: (1) Devotion to family

And so on through the remaining list. Then, conduct a third round on the ones you did not select in round one to prioritize those values, much like in a double-elimination tournament bracket. Just because these were not selected in the first round does not mean they are not of high value, and may bubble back into the upper tier of values in subsequent rounds.

Continue the process until you have completed sorting your list of values. When finished, you should have a set of higher priority and lower priority values. You may be surprised to learn what you value most.

6. Your Personal Code of Character

The following Personal Code of Character draws all the elements of "The ABC Model" together. It consists of a written Code of Character produced from the Code of Character Worksheet that follows.

After learning "The ABC Model", first complete your Personal Code of Character Worksheet. The worksheet provides a means to list your beliefs, values, principles and ideals, map them to your 10 Core Virtues, and draw statements that connect your ethics with your virtues, revealing your character.

The following examples demonstrate how to use the worksheet to produce a comprehensive, consistent Personal Code of Character.

Code of Character Worksheet Example

Begin by using the Code of Character Worksheet (free download in Microsoft Excel format at www.eIntegrity.net).

Begin by listing your beliefs under the Ethics column. The example below uses generic belief systems, such as the Golden Rule. Be more specific and detailed. For instance, if you subscribe to the 10 Commandments, then list each. It is best to create your own list of those beliefs that are relevant to you. It is not necessary that they come from any formal ethics system.

	ETHICS	CHARACTER	VIRTUES									
	Beliefs	**Code of Character**	Justice	Temperance	Prudence	Courage	Honesty	Trust	Discipline	Faith	Hope	Love
1	The Golden Rule		x						x			x
2	10 Commandments	Live a principled life.		x	x		x			x		
3	Conscience	Believe in and do what I know in my heart is right, just and good.	x	x	x	x	x	x	x	x		
4	Creed					x			x	x	x	
5	Doctrines							x		x		
6	The Law				x				x			
7	Code of Ethics		x	x	x	x	x	x	x	x	x	x

Next, map your beliefs to your virtues by placing an "x" under each Virtues column where you currently either employ or will need to utilize that virtue to bring the belief to life through your actions and behavior. Remember, this is your personal code, so others may not select the same matchings as yours.

Finally, write a brief statement under the Character column where you have a strong commitment to a particular virtue-ethic. This should be a succinct but descriptive expression of a character trait. These will become your "codes" of character. It is not necessary to write a code for every belief. Perhaps a dozen codes, more or less, will be sufficient. The list should contain those character traits most pertinent to you.

Repeat the process for your values. You may want to list all your beliefs, values and principles and ideals before mapping them to virtues and writing your codes.

ETHICS	CHARACTER	VIRTUES									
Values	Code of Character	Justice	Temperance	Prudence	Courage	Honesty	Trust	Discipline	Faith	Hope	Love
1 Education								x		x	
2 Family	Value the relationships and things that are genuine, especially love of family.			x							x
3 Happiness	Live a life of wholeness, completeness, true happiness	x	x	x	x	x	x	x	x	x	x
4 Health			x	x				x			
5 Liberty		x			x						x
6 Life	Never forget life is a gift and be grateful for it each and every day.							x			x
7 Truth	Be honest, trustworthy and disciplined in all my dealings.					x	x				
8 Beauty											x

Repeat the process for your principles.

ETHICS	CHARACTER	VIRTUES									
Principles	Code of Character	Justice	Temperance	Prudence	Courage	Honesty	Trust	Discipline	Faith	Hope	Love
1 Accountability	Have moral fiber and courage of character.	x	x	x	x			x			
2 Commitment	Live my life with justice, wisdom, courage and self-control.							x			
3 Duty					x	x		x			
4 Excellence	Pursue and achieve noble ideals and goals with excellence.							x			
5 Fairness					x						
6 Respect	Be the genuine me with pure motives and good habits.					x	x				
7 Responsibility	Accept responsibility for my actions and life.				x	x	x	x			

Finally, identify your ideals and goals in a similar manner.

ETHICS	CHARACTER	Justice	Temperance	Prudence	Courage	Honesty	Trust	Discipline	Faith	Hope	Love
Ideals	**Code of Character**										
1 Charity	Grow spiritually through faith, hope and charity.										x
2 Honor								x			
3 Joy									x		
4 Kindness											x
5 Patience				x							
6 Peace							x	x			
7 Success		x	x	x	x	x	x	x	x	x	x
8 Humility						x					
9 Wisdom				x							

You may go back and refine your worksheet numerous times before you are satisfied. The process of doing this exercise has significant merit in helping you make an inventory of your ethics and relating them to your actions and behaviors.

Once you complete the worksheet, you will have a set of codes that you may document in a Personal Code of Character, such as the example that follows.

Preamble (Example)

I place ultimate value on attaining and sustaining personal integrity. I acknowledge that integrity will require commitment, discipline, and considerable effort. Because I have high standards and expectations of myself, I commit myself to a course of excellence and honor.

To guide me in my life of integrity, I pledge and commit myself to:

1. Never forget life is a gift and be grateful for it each and every day.
2. Believe in and do what I know in my heart is right, just and good.
3. Value the relationships and things that are genuine, especially love of family.
4. Live a principled life.

5. Pursue and achieve noble ideals and goals with excellence.
6. Live my life with justice, wisdom, courage and self-control.
7. Be honest, trustworthy and disciplined in all my dealings.
8. Grow spiritually through faith, hope and charity.
9. Be the genuine me with pure motives and good habits.
10. Have moral fiber and courage of character.
11. Accept responsibility and accountability for my actions and life.
12. Live a life of wholeness, completeness, true happiness.

At the beginning of each week, I will reflect upon my character and integrity by reviewing my Code of Character. I will strive to have wholeness, completeness and consistency in how I think, what I do, why I do it, and who I am.

My Code of Character (Example)

1. **Never forget life is a gift and be grateful for it each and every day.**

   Life is an immense blessing. I will be grateful and thankful for the privilege to be alive and have opportunities to be and do what is best. I will not waste a single day, for each moment is extremely precious.

2. **Believe in and do what I know in my heart is right, just and good.**

   My thoughts and actions will always be based upon justice, truth, and what ought to be. I will not be lazy in thought or late in acting.

3. **Value the relationships and things that are genuine, especially love of family.**

   Relationships and material possessions are what I make them; good or bad. I will honor and enrich the loving relationships in my life, especially my family and friends. That means I will make time for them. I will either correct or terminate relationships that are unhealthy. I will not accumulate material things to make me happy. Happiness comes from within my soul, my character and my integrity.

4. Live a principled life.

The "north star" of principles will guide me. I will not be veered off course by "shiny objects" or temptations. I will stay upon the course to integrity.

5. Pursue and achieve noble ideals and goals with excellence.

Life is short. I will devote my time, energy and resources to achieve noble goals. Whatever I set out to do, I will do it with all the capacities I have, and demonstrate excellence in my work and accomplishments.

6. Live my life with justice, wisdom, courage and self-control.

I will live by the time-honored moral virtues. I will make it a habit to be just, wise, strong and in control of my emotions. I will treat others as I want to be treated (The Golden Rule).

I will be kind and courteous, for there is never a valid reason for being rude. I will honor the dignity, rights and freedoms of all humans.

7. Be honest, trustworthy and disciplined in all my dealings.

I will be true to myself and others by being honest, trustworthy, and disciplined. I will live with an appropriate level of transparency so others will know who I am. I will keep my word, honor my commitments, and fulfill my obligations.

8. Grow spiritually through faith, hope and charity.

I am a spiritual being and will grow in faith, hope, charity and love. I will be optimistic and positive as much as is reasonable. I will work to earn the respect of my family, friends and peers, and perhaps serve as an inspiration for them to follow their own path to integrity.

9. Be the genuine me with pure motives and good habits.

I will not "play games" in my conduct with people, operate from false motives, have my own selfish agenda in my dealings or be hypocritical. I will strengthen my healthy habits, and eliminate my destructive habits. I will not change who I am to please others. I will not allow my bad moods to influence my behavior.

10. Have moral fiber and courage of character.

I will be strong in the face of wrong, even when it is unpopular.

11. Accept responsibility and accountability for my actions and life.

I will not play "the blame game". I will take full responsibility and accountability for my actions. If I fail, I will confess my failing without trying to avoid past responsibility or cover up my mistakes. I will learn from my mistakes and failings. I will live by my ethics and virtues to keep me from making future mistakes that can be avoided with moral character and integrity.

12. Live a life of wholeness, completeness, true happiness.

I will live a balanced life with appropriate attention to work, play and rest. I will be neither a workaholic nor lazy. I realize that happiness is not a destination, but comes from the journey to integrity.

Conclusion

My Personal Code of Character will serve as a guide to my path when I face ethical dilemmas. As I grow, I may need to revise and amend this Code of Character. This is the covenant with my soul to be a person of integrity.

7. Your Integrity LifeMap

Ten Actions to Achieving/Improving Integrity

Action 1: Study and understand the integrity framework (The ABC Model)

Action 2: Develop a matrix of your ethics, virtues and character. (See Examples)

Action 3: Extract from the matrix your own "Code of Character"

Action 4: Review your Code frequently to reinforce your ideals

Action 5: Compare your recent behaviors/actions that are inconsistent with your Code

Action 6: Note any of your behaviors/actions that are inconsistent with your Code

Action 7: Determine what or how you should have responded which would have been consistent with your Code, and which principles, values, ideals and virtues you lacked

Action 8: Identify any traits or habits you could develop to support your Code

Action 9: Practice developing those habits/traits

Action 10: Repeat actions 4 through 9 on a regular basis

Epilogue

"Integrity can be neither lost nor concealed
nor faked nor quenched nor artificially come by nor
outlived,
nor, I believe, in the long run, denied."
~ Eudora Welty[28]

"Three Steps to Integrity: The ABC Model" is the result of my journey seeking an answer to one simple, but painfully elusive question: "What is integrity, and how can you achieve it?" My intention was not to expand on the philosophers and theologians. My goal was to get, for my own understanding, a simple conceptual model of what integrity is.

Drawing upon my Judeo-Christian background, I read the works of the Greek Philosophers; Old Testament Prophets; New Testament Theologians; and Modern Psychologists. I read the related writings from Islamic, Eastern and Native American traditions. I drew deeply from the reservoirs of contemporary writers, including Stephen L. Carter, Stephen Covey, Deepak Chopra, Peter Diamandis, D. Joseph Jacques, Theodore Malloch, Christopher Panza and others whom I mention in the pages of this book.

At the end of this quest, the stubborn question remained: "BUT, what IS integrity?" The brilliant minds have dealt with all aspects of integrity, but for me, no one placed all the moving parts of integrity together into a comprehensive whole, in the same way puzzle pieces fit together to form a picture.

Frustrated, I wrote the individual components of integrity (ethics, honesty, virtues, character, courage, and so on, thirty in all) on separate index cards. Then, I threw the thirty cards on the table, and began trying to organize them.

After five years of trial and error, testing various models for consistency, the cards finally "fell into place". I know more fully the elusive nature of defining and more importantly, achieving integrity.

I now have the model of integrity that makes sense for me.

"Three Steps to Integrity: The ABC Model" is my way of sharing that simple model with you.

The model is easy to understand, but as with most things of true value in life, achieving integrity requires commitment and discipline. There are tremendous rewards for living a life of integrity: wholeness, completeness, happiness, success, peace, excellence and knowledge.

Don Quixote in "Man of La Mancha" put into words, immortalized in "The Impossible Dream", the meaning of his life's quest.

"To dream ... the impossible dream
To fight ... the unbeatable foe
To bear ... with unbearable sorrow
To run ... where the brave dare not go
To right ... the unrightable wrong
To love ... pure and chaste from afar
To try ... when your arms are too weary
To reach ... the unreachable star.

This is my quest, to follow that star
No matter how hopeless, no matter how far
To fight for the right, without question or pause
To be willing to march into Hell, for a Heavenly cause

And I know if I'll only be true, to this glorious quest,
That my heart will lie peaceful and calm,
when I'm laid to my rest ...
And the world will be better for this:
That one man, scorned and covered with scars,
Still strove, with his last ounce of courage,
To reach ... the unreachable star."

"To Dream the Impossible Dream" Man of La Mancha (1972)
Mitch Leigh and Joe Darion

I challenge you to set about on your own quest for integrity. May you have the desire to perfect yourself and discover the vitality of a virtuous life; and may you find the abundant life integrity provides.

What can ONE person do?

You can be the spark that helps to start a new revival of ethics, virtues, character and integrity. Your journey to live a life of integrity will inspire others to join us.

Any dead fish can float downstream. It takes a strong salmon to fight upstream, to go against the mainstream, to be ONE.

In 1920, Robert Frost wrote a poem that illustrates how being an individual who takes the less traveled road can make all the difference in life.

The Road Not Taken

Two roads diverged in a yellow wood,
And sorry I could not travel both
And be one traveler, long I stood
And looked down one as far as I could
To where it bent in the undergrowth;

Then took the other, as just as fair,
And having perhaps the better claim,
Because it was grassy and wanted wear;
Though as for that the passing there
Had worn them really about the same,

And both that morning equally lay
In leaves no step had trodden black.
Oh, I kept the first for another day!
Yet knowing how way leads on to way,
I doubted if I should ever come back.

I shall be telling this with a sigh
Somewhere ages and ages hence:
Two roads diverged in a wood, and I—
I took the one less traveled by,
And that has made all the difference.

About the author

Dr. William L. "Bill" Jenkins

Educator, Information Technology Manager, Minister, Author, Historian.

Bill Jenkins grew up in Mississippi during the 1960s Civil Rights Era. He earned a Bachelor of Science in Education degree from Delta State University, where he did his student teaching at an all African-American high school in the Mississippi Delta in 1969. This began a lifelong passion for social justice. Bill received his Master of Divinity degree from Southern Seminary, and earned his Doctorate at Columbia Theological Seminary near Atlanta where his dissertation focused on the use of technology in churches. He conducted additional graduate information technology study through the University of Southern Mississippi and NASA's Stennis Space Center. Dr. Jenkins taught graduate technology management and business courses at San Diego State University, Webster University and National University. Jenkins has 40+ years in ministry. He founded an urban ministry center in San Diego, California. Bill served over a decade as manager of IT Operations at one of Southern California's largest and most progressive water agencies. His department won several prominent awards, including the 2008 "Best of California" award for Excellence in IT Operations, Support and Service, presented by The Center for Digital Government; and was a two-time winner of the Excellence in IT Practices award from the Municipal Information Systems Association of California (MISAC). Dr. Jenkins cofounded The Integrity Network (eIntegrity.net) in response to the collapse of integrity in our financial, governmental, and business institutions.

Drawing from his theology training, practical business and higher education experience, Bill created "The ABC Model", a simple, comprehensive framework for understanding integrity's components; a tool for achieving integrity in personal and public life.

Cited References

Authors and Books

[1] Carter, Stephen L., *Integrity*, Harper Perennial Publishers, 1996.

[2] Chopra, Deepak, *War of the Worldviews: Science vs. Spirituality*, Center Point, 2012.

[3] Collins, Jim, *Good to Great: Why Some Companies Make the Leap...and Others Don't*, HarperCollins Publishers, 2001.

[4] Covey, Stephen, *The 7 Habits of Highly Effective People: Powerful Lessons in Personal Change*, Free Press, 2004 (Updated).

[5] Covey, Stephen M. R., *The Speed of Trust: The One Thing That Changes Everything*, Free Press, 2008 (Reprint).

[6] Diamandis, Peter, *Abundance: The Future Is Better Than You Think*, Free Press, 2012.

[7] Fletcher, Joseph, *Situation Ethics: The New Morality*, Westminster Press, 1966.

[8] Fulghum, Robert, *All I Really Need to Know I Learned in Kindergarten*, Random House Publishing Group, 1988.

[9] Greer, Ronald J., *If You Know Who You Are, You'll Know What To Do*, Abingdon Press, 2009.

[10] Jacques, D. Joseph, *Chivalry-Now: The Code of Male Ethics*, John Hunt Publishing, 2010.

[11] Josephson, Michael, *Parenting to Build Character in Your Teen: Teach Your Teens the Six Pillars of Character!*, Boys Town Press, 2001.

[12] Kotler, Steven, *Abundance: The Future Is Better Than You Think*, Free Press, 2012.

[13] Kouzes, James, *The Leadership Challenge, 4th Edition*, Jossey-Bass, 2007.

[14] Lewis, C.S., *Mere Christianity*, HarperCollins Publishers, 2001 (Reprint).

[15] Malloch, Theodore R., *Doing Virtuous Business: The Remarkable Success of Spiritual Enterprise*, Thomas Nelson, Inc., 2011.

[16] Maxwell, John C., *Be All You Can Be: A Challenge to Stretch Your God-Given Potential*, David C. Cook Publishers, 2007.

[17] Merrill, Rebecca R., *The Speed of Trust: The One Thing That Changes Everything*, Free Press, 2008 (Reprint)

[18] Mlodinow, Leonard, *War of the Worldviews: Science vs. Spirituality*, Center Point, 2012.

[19] Oates, Wayne E., *Anxiety in Christian Experience*, Word Press, 1974.

[20] Panza, Christopher, *Ethics For Dummies*, John Wiley & Sons, Incorporated, 2011.

[21] Peck, M. Scott, *The Road Less Traveled: A New Psychology of Love, Traditional Values and Spiritual Growth*, Touchstone, 2003 (25th Anniversary Edition).

[22] Posner, Barry, *The Leadership Challenge, 4th Edition*, Jossey-Bass, 2007.

[23] Potthast, Adam, *Ethics For Dummies*, John Wiley & Sons, Incorporated, 2011.

[24] Solomon, Robert C., *A Better Way to Think About Business: How Personal Integrity Leads to Corporate Success*, Oxford University Press, 1999.

Websites and Online Quotations

[25] BrainyQuote.com

[26] Merriam-Webster.com

[27] ScienceDaily.com

[28] ThinkExist.com

[29] QuotationsBook.com

[30] QuoteGarden.com

[31] Wikipedia.org

[32] Wikiquote.org

CF 'IA information can be obtained at www.ICGtesting.com
Pr   d in the USA
BV   /032224121112

3051 '3BV00009B/1/P